LOVE, IMPERFECTLY KNOWN

Dear John,

It was so nice to meet you. With all my gratitude and brotherly affection,

J. Emmanuel

emmanuel @ taye. fr

Love, Imperfectly Known

Beyond Spontaneous Representations of God

BROTHER EMMANUEL, OF TAIZÉ
Translated by Dinah Livingstone

continuum

Published by the Continuum International Publishing Group

The Tower Building	80 Maiden Lane
11 York Road	Suite 704
London	New York
SE1 7NX	NY 10038

www.continuumbooks.com

First published in English in 2011

British Library Cataloguing-in-Publication Data
A catalogue record for this book is available from the British Library.

ISBN 978-1-4411-1637-6

Typeset by Fakenham Photosetting Ltd, Fakenham, Norfolk NR21 8LQ
Printed and bound in India

Contents

Foreword

The Romans said it: books have a history of their own. Brother Emmanuel's book has one too. Knowing this history will show how rigorous his research has been. And this will make the book's meaning clearer.

A young man seeking the absolute wanted to carry on this search in the common life of a monastery. He had often heard Brother Roger tell his brothers or visitors to Taizé: 'God can only love.' Repeating this was a way of constantly trying to convince those seeking God that in him there could only be love. From his youth, Brother Roger himself must have been extremely sensitive to how a certain way of speaking about God, though well-intentioned, sometimes set up barriers against trusting him and even gave rise to pain and doubt.

Brother Emmanuel knew well that this imperfectly understood love of God had first of all to shine through an authentic life, but at the same time he was driven to try to overcome the intellectual obstacles placed in his way. That required continuing, relentless work. Because he had to be as rigorous as possible.

Of course, his closeness to Brother Roger and his life shared with his brother monks profoundly affected his reflection. But because he had to go into barely explored areas, his work necessarily had to be personal and could not expect to involve the whole community. The difficulty in producing this book was this: challenging spontaneous representations of God involved always passing from one sphere to another, drawing provisional conclusions and then revising them, refusing to believe an end had been reached.

So the history of this book is not yet finished. The exploration continues. Speaking adequately about God will always be beyond us. But in order to be understood when we speak about him, we must listen again and again to the questions raised by our own time, while remembering that the experience of centuries remains a treasure upon which we can rely.

Brother François, of Taizé

Introduction

Whether we call ourselves 'believers', 'non-believers', 'seekers' or simply 'open-minded', all of us are influenced by unconscious psychological projections when the question of God arises. For some these projections will lead to revolt, rejection, fear or indifference. For others, these projections will give rise to a representation of God that blocks or hampers access to discoveries that are essential to the blossoming of an inner life. These unconscious processes often work against a search for meaning or spiritual experience. By unmasking that unconscious influence on the most widespread of these spontaneous representations of God, this book invites each reader to look again at the existential and spiritual questions, which are both the most universal and the most intimate, so as to conceive, discover or rediscover a love imperfectly understood.

'Love, imperfectly known': We are not talking about an unknown love. Who has never heard, albeit indirectly, of the possible existence of a God of love, of divine love? Rather, we are talking about a love that is known badly because it is constantly disfigured. After suffering an ordeal, many people can no longer bear to hear the word 'God' and even less can they bear the mention of an all-loving God, whose existence seems incompatible to them with a world where evil reigns. How could an all-loving God have wanted or allowed all the various kinds of evil from which human beings suffer? The difficulty, impossibility even, of believing in a God of love because of evil in the world remains one of the foundations of modern atheism, the first objection raised against any theological proposition. This confrontation with suffering is also the principal cause of rebellion or doubt by believers, who are tempted to suspect the divine will of conniving with evil. In both cases, this inner battle makes it difficult to connect the mystery of love with a possible divine mystery. Every quest for meaning or any spiritual experience has to face that challenge at some point. It is the first hurdle to overcome or at least an obligatory stage that must be covered in any journey that is setting out to be clear and realistic. That is why the first part of this book is devoted entirely to this question. It is not afraid of broaching the kinds of evil usually ascribed to a Creator-God, that is to say, natural disasters, diseases and finally, death. Neither is it afraid of stressing the vital support that human sciences and exact sciences can bring to such an investigation, by pointing out convergences between scientific observations and theological research. The book exposes the human desire for omnipotence that is present from infancy and has an effect on our spontaneous representations of divine omnipotence, so that it conditions our personal ideas about the problem of evil from the outset.

This first part of the book invites everyone – believer or non-believer – not to remain dependent on that conditioning. It leads the reader to reconsider the apparent incompatibility between the existence of an omnipotent God of love and a world where evil reigns.

When doubt and rebellion in the face of evil are no longer insuperable obstacles, the main hurdles in a quest for meaning or spiritual experience lie in secret fears enmeshed in the idea of God. Every human being has fears, whether unconscious or no, recognised or unacknowledged, accepted or rejected. They can extend from the simple fear of being disappointed or misunderstood to the fear of being unloved or abandoned. The most disturbing fears arise directly or indirectly from the difficulty each of us has in believing ourselves worthy of being loved. The root of this difficulty lies in the deep sense of guilt, inherent in the discovery in ourselves of disconcerting traits, particularly, aggressive impulses, sexual or otherwise, that foster an inner uneasiness. The somewhat harsh judgment resulting from this difficult self-confrontation is often unconsciously projected onto a God perceived by so many –

believers and non-believers – as the being who might not love them because of their most disturbing traits, or even judge them harshly, punish or reject them. There are many kinds of religious indifference, behind which lie such secret terrors of God. There are also many religious practices where these same fears feed an inner life that is stymied rather than blossoming. The second part of the book tries to promote a better self-understanding, in particular of the different stages of psychological development at the origin of these impulses that are sometimes so disturbing. It encourages a reconciliation with ourselves by taking a clear and kindly look to correct the harshness unconsciously projected onto spontaneous representations of divine judgment. This part of the book looks at the secret wounds we all bear, which give rise to many attitudes judged – rightly or wrongly – to be reprehensible and then asks how a God of love would regard these wounds. In this way, it opens up an idea of divine judgment that is far removed from what our human imagination might conceive, following a difficult self-confrontation.

If you are afraid of someone, you do not want to approach them or get to know them better. Overcoming certain secret fears about God raises the question of an inner life or spiritual experience more urgently. The development and flowering of an inner life comes up against a huge obstacle: divine transcendence is generally accompanied by the spontaneous representation of a distant, domineering or condescending Being. Such representations of God often make some people lose interest in spiritual experience. Or it leads others to conduct a master–slave relationship between dominator and dominated. The considerable repercussions lead us to question the psychic origins of this natural tendency to perceive transcendence or divine greatness in this way. By showing the various transferences or projections feeding the representation of a domineering or distant God, the third part of this book invites the reader to ponder the radical change of perspective gained by the presentation of a God who, according to Christian revelation, wishes to come very close to each of us, a God who wants to love his creature intensely and be intensely loved. Just as any sincere demand to be loved

has something overwhelming about it, so the realisation of the
existence of such a divine expectation upsets many ways of
apprehending the question of God or leading an inner life. It also
invites each of us to look differently on our own capacity to love.
This book gradually reveals the true foundations of confidence
in this reciprocal divine–human love, to which so many mystical
traditions have borne witness throughout the ages, and which, for
Christian mysticism, is the heart and culmination of any spiritual
quest

For those who consciously engage in this reciprocal divine–
human love and those who continue to reject any religious
belief, mental images of God arising through the inevitable use
of human analogies – the father figure, for example – release
unconscious projections, linked to their personal history, their
psychological profile and their sexual identity. Under the influence
of this ever-active process, some people will keep their distance
from a God who reminds them only too well of the unhealed
wounds from their childhood or youth. Others will systematically reject any spiritual perspective, which they have made the
scapegoat for a personal settling of scores. Others still will only
lead their inner lives through the prism of the single analogy
they have retained from their religious education or surrounding
culture, with this double risk: either the analogy involved is
linked, consciously or unconsciously to a negative experience in
their lives, and so does not allow their relationship to God to
go beyond a certain degree of confidence and intimacy; or the
analogy involved is linked, consciously or unconsciously, to a
positive experience and therefore may foster a concept of God
reduced to that aspect alone, to the detriment of other aspects
that may characterise the divine mystery. This means that any
quest for meaning or spiritual experience needs to take care with
any human analogies used in so much that is said about God.
First, we must step back from the cultural, psychological and
theological conditioning, whose marks they bear. Then we must
be clear about their advantages and disadvantages, in order to
free ourselves from spontaneous representations of God whose
exclusive link with this or that analogy prevents access to other

aspects of the mystery of a God who is love. The importance of doing this cannot be underestimated, because the power of the mental image associated with the notion of God influences each person's convictions and the conduct of each person's inner life. We need only set two analogies side by side, which, despite being somewhat provocative and a bit of a caricature, at least convey the power of the mental image and its repercussions in terms of personal interest, response, confidence and tenderness. Their inner disposition will be very different according to whether people think they are in the presence of a bearded old man, with a severe expression and authoritarian gestures; or in the presence of a charming, welcoming and smiling young woman.

The fourth part of this book analyses cultural, psychological and theological forms of conditioning, which may harm us all. It invites the reader not to remain dependent on an exclusively masculine approach to God, to recognise the appropriateness of feminine analogies, which reflect the beauty of divine love. In doing so, this part of the book is an invitation both to those who think of themselves as non-believers and those who are already consciously living a spiritual life. It appeals to the former not to take up a religious position based on a reductionist representation of God, which may have been instilled in them from childhood or fostered by caricatures belonging to their cultural environment. It appeals to the latter not to prevent a God of love from leading them even further along the way of intimacy with himself, offering them his divine love in the way he judges best suited to each person to experience the most intense and beautiful union of the divine and human possible.

This new way of looking at existential and spiritual questions, which are both the most universal and the most intimate, offers support to any quest for the ultimate meaning of life, the ultimate meaning of love. That will have repercussions on daily life, particularly the loving words and actions that may take place in it. Whatever their religious convictions, in their own experience of love many people feel a mystery that goes beyond them and points them indirectly towards an ultimate meaning. But fewer of them realise how that ultimate meaning could give them a way of renewing and even intensifying that love day after day. At a time when the quality of love exchanged in daily life is regarded more highly than social, family or any other considerations that might have prevailed in the past, one of the great challenges remains the quest for a strengthening of love over the long term, since even the most full-flowering love is never once and for all and it may fade with time. This book's epilogue goes to the heart of what human love can find as motivation and inner strength by welcoming the ultimate meaning of life and the ultimate meaning of love, as Christian mysticism conceives them. Contrary to many received ideas, Christian mysticism is capable of allowing for the reconciliation of daily life with an inner life, of loving actions with the quest for the ultimate, of sexuality with spirituality, of erotic passion with mystical aspiration. It gives a meaning to life and a meaning to love that is high enough for anyone to draw from it the motivation and inner strength to help a natural inclination, which would be incapable, on its own, of making love last over the long term, much less of strengthening it. This ultimate meaning gives loving words and gestures a value, supporting the renewal day by day, in the deepest self, of what is really essential, a renewal without which no love can learn truly to love, blossom and transfigure time. Then that enemy synonymous with love's falling off might be transformed into a real ally. By allowing that continual renewal of the essential, which is only possible over the long term, it becomes a gift to reciprocal love, so that it tends, day after day towards its highest degree of intensity. At the same time, these final pages of the book will plunge into the heart of divine–human love, into the hidden face and secret springs of the monastic absolute. The monk is also called to a reciprocal love, taking seriously the divine Presence continually with him and preparing inwardly to welcome its love and to love in return with all the fibres of his being. It reveals the importance of the daily integration of his humanity, his feelings, his sexual identity, his way of being and loving, an integration which alone can transfigure his yearning to be loved and to love. In the language of love he addresses to God the intense passion called 'Eros' that dwells in every human being indirectly reveals his true identity and ultimate destiny.

PART 1

Does Evil Contradict the Existence of a God of Love?

Unconscious Projections and Representations of Divine Omnipotence

Many people think that the human race would never have had to face such a problem of evil if an omnipotent God really existed. How could such a God have wanted or even allowed the slightest form of evil? Why did he not create a world that was better from many points of view? It is not surprising that such arguments have led some to doubt the existence of a God of love and others to remain imprisoned in theological representations that are as incoherent as they are revolting, in particular, a two-faced God who, on the one hand, claims to love humanity and, on the other, wants or permits evil to happen. Neither is it surprising that many philosophers and theologians have not succeeded in overcoming the contradictions inherent in this problem, because this is not just a question of intelligence or knowledge. Unconscious psychological determinisms are also involved and if they are not carefully identified and dealt with, they will keep this impression of an apparently irreconcilable incompatibility between the various manifestations of evil and the existence of an omnipotent God of love.

By looking at the way in which this feeling of incompatibility forms in the consciousness, the first part of the book will point out the considerable influence of the unconscious projection of the human desire for omnipotence onto spontaneous representations of divine omnipotence. As the repercussions of this psychological projection are gradually unmasked, the reader will be invited to look in an entirely new way at the apparent incompatibility between the existence of an omnipotent God of love and a world in which evil reigns.

Love, Imperfectly Known 978-1-4411-1637-6
Published by The Continuum International Publishing Group

**The publishers greatly regret that the following errors and
omissions were made in this title:**

p.xiv, l.32: "welcome its love and to love in return" should read
"welcome her love and love her in return"

p.1, l.2: "omnipotent God" should read "omnipotent God of love"

p.4, l.11: "and" should read "or"

p.6, l.1: "risk" should read "risk of suffering deeply from"

p.6, l.8: "the creature suffering profoundly" should read "God suffering profoundly"

p.6, l.12: "love can exist" should read "evil can exist"

p.7, l.22-3: "this or that woman" should read "this man or that woman"

p.10, l.21: "project" should read "projection"

p.21, l.12: "Apart from these questions" should read "Apart from these
questions and their possible consequences in peoples'
convictions"

p.22, l.24: "look" should read "change our way of looking"

p.39, l.7: "elements" should read "elements, including the most obscure
aspects of their psyche"

p.42, l.10: "language" should read "body language"

p.42, l.22-3: "towards finding his own goal and finding himself" should read
"against finding his own goal and himself"

p.46, l.32-3: "of a person with whom" should read "of their being with which"

p.51, l.15: "God." should read "God, from which their convictions
are forged."

p.62, l.7: "certain evangelical theology" should read "theology that is
consistent with the Gospel"

p.67, l.4: "mediations" should read "meditations"

p.73, l.10: "neighbour" should read "neighbour, the choice to love and
constantly to grow in love,"

p.87, l.31: "to be loved" should read "to be loved and to love"

p.109, n.b: "Wis :2" should read "Wis 8:2"

p.112, n.a: should read "Vocabulaire de théologie biblique, op. cit. p. 968"

p.113, n.e: "Lk 9:2-10" should read "Lk 19:2-10"

p.124, l.2: "he is a Person" should read "she is a Person"

p.125, l.10: "Holy Spirit its place" should read "Holy Spirit her place"

p.132, n.a: "IV 17,4" should read "IV, 7,4"

p.139, l.25: "to welcome this love and to love it in return" should read
　　　　　　"to welcome her love and to love her in return"

p.140, l.6-7: "what is in" should read "all the feelings within"

p.140, l.7: "it is able to welcome the love this heart offers it in all its intensity"
　　　　　　should read "she is able to welcome the love this heart offers her
　　　　　　in all its intensity"

p.140, l.16: "that knowing such signs" should read "that such signs"

p.140, l.17: "very" should read "very rarely addressed to God"

p.140, l.25: "God's yearning to be loved" should read
　　　　　　"the yearning to be loved by God"

p.140, l.28: "God's yearning to love" should read
　　　　　　"the yearning to love God"

p.141, l.10: "we must love with all the force of Eros" should read
　　　　　　"we must love God with all the force of Eros"

p.143, n.5: "gropings" should read "gropings of evolution"

p.145, n.12: "perfect state" should read "ideal state"

p.160, n.76: "infantilising father" should read "infantilising faith"

p.164, n.90: "five hundred" should read "one hundred and fifty"

p.165, n.91: "familiarly" should read "as 'You'"

p.166, n.98: "illustrate" should read "counterbalance"
　　　　　　"difficult" should read "dry"

p.170, n.104: "accompanies them" should read "accompanies him"

p.172, n.112: "mystery of love and" should read "mystery of love, that,"

p.173, n.118: "serious" should read "serious commitment"

p.173, n.119: "love oneself" should read "love each other"
　　　　　　"discover oneself" should read "discover each other"
　　　　　　"to love to love" should read "to love her or him"

p.176, n.124: "Jer 17:19" should read "Ps 7:9"
　　　　　　"how much he loves" should read "how much he loves her"
　　　　　　"cannot see or touch it" should read "cannot see or touch her"
　　　　　　"human being has for it" should read "human being has for her"

Beyond the Desire for Omnipotence

In a quest for meaning in the face of the harsh reality of evil, the representation that each of us spontaneously makes of divine omnipotence can influence our personal convictions much more than we might suspect. In order to discover the scope of this influence we need first to recognise the unconscious conditioning caused by dreams of omnipotence lurking in every human being. A secret yearning to become omnipotent takes possession of the depths of the psyche from infancy onwards, when the discovery of his or her own limitations makes the infant want to gain the power to fulfil the slightest desire immediately. That wish may then lead the human mind to represent divine omnipotence in terms of the omnipotence to which it unconsciously aspires from infancy. At the heart of his research on belief and unbelief, the psychologist Antoine Vergote stresses the influence of this infantile desire for omnipotence and notes the thought of Sigmund Freud on the most common representations of divine omnipotence: 'Human beings delegate to God the task of operating the omnipotence of which they feel deprived. Hence the omnipotent God is the reflection of the imaginary omnipotence of our desires.'[a] This desire for omnipotence becomes, among other things, the unconscious desire to be able to exercise absolute control over

---

a   *Religion, foi, incroyance, étude psychologique*, Brussels, Mardaga, 1987, p. 217.

every life, so that the psychological projection of this desire also conditions the spontaneous human representation of the divine will. The unconscious aspiration towards absolute control drives him to consider that the events of his own life, the lives of those close to him or anyone else, are wanted, controlled or even imposed from on high by this divine Being. The more active this unconscious projection is, the less it allows the individual to distinguish between the divine will and what actually happens in his or her own life or the lives of others. That is why every kind of evil, every misfortune whether distant or close to home, leads him or her to doubt the existence of a God of love and the quality of a divine love suspected of conniving with evil. But this is also the reason why that doubt and suspicion ought to be seriously challenged. It appears that both arise from a psychic process that is still very dependent on the unconscious projection of an infantile desire for omnipotence onto God.

When we can assess how much our own unconscious aspiration towards a form of absolute control can distort from the outset the representation of God upon which we develop all our reflection on the problem of evil, we discover one of the most precious contributions psychology can offer to inner development. We learn to take into account the role of certain unconscious determinisms in the formation of a natural religiosity, from which most of our spontaneous representations of God derive. This natural religiosity conditions the representations of God, upon which both a certain kind of popular faith and a certain kind of atheist reasoning are based. Both are invited to step back from these representations of God by becoming aware of the role of these unconscious determinisms. Avoiding both blind adhesion and simplistic reduction of religion to an illusion forged by the unconscious, we owe it to ourselves to distinguish this basis of natural religiosity from an authentic spiritual quest that tries to tackle the great existential questions without remaining trapped by harmful unconscious projections.

Human Freedom Fully Respected

The difficulty of applying this discernment to belief in an omnipotent God of love arises from the fact that the unconscious projection of the infantile desire for omnipotence took over the depths of the human psyche at the time when it was at its most malleable. The hold of this psychological projection makes it almost impossible to acquire a means of discernment capable of illuminating any quest for meaning in the face of various manifestations of evil. Seeking a God who is love in his essence means being careful no longer to represent this divine omnipotence in terms of the human desire for omnipotence, because this belief is not about any omnipotence but about the omnipotence of divine love.[a1] This distinction challenges an all-too-human conception of omnipotence, by suggesting that we redefine the notion of divine omnipotence in terms of the most fundamental characteristics of the mystery of love.

Within the framework of a mature relationship, there can be no doubt that one of the most essential characteristics of the mystery of love is respect for the freedom of the person loved, starting from respect for his or her decision whether to engage in the relationship at all. Anyone who has experienced the miracle of genuine love, even if it was only once in a lifetime, knows very well that it would have been unthinkable to impose one's own feelings,

---

a   These numbers refer to the Notes section at the end of the book.

to force the other to accept them, at the risk of possibly being refused. If human love can go that far, it seems inconceivable that divine love can do anything less. Therefore when we think about this existence of a God of love, we have to take into account the respect he would show for human freedom. Such a God would not force his creature to live in a harmonious relationship with himself or to contribute to the happiness of his environment, even though that might mean the creature suffering profoundly from wrong choices made in the exercise of freedom. This realisation leads to the complete reversal of the usual objection to any belief in a God of love: the fact that human beings can freely refuse to love and hence that love can exist not only overcomes this objection but considerably reinforces the possibility of a link between the mystery of love and the mystery of God. Because of this respect for human freedom, it becomes no longer impossible for evil to manifest itself here below and, paradoxically, possible that its manifestation becomes fully compatible with the existence of a God of love!

A God *who* Does *not* Want *or* Permit Evil

This astonishing change of perspective challenges in many ways the apparent incompatibility between the existence of evil and that of a God of love. It also prevents us from constantly misrepresenting God's will, when we interpret certain trials that beset each of our lives or the lives of those near to us. The more seriously we take the bad impact of human freedom on all areas of life, the weaker becomes the tendency systematically to link the divine will with tragedies in our lives or the lives of those dear to us. We become careful no longer to remain dependent on the projection of the infantile desire for omnipotence, which unconsciously feeds the representation of a Dictator God manipulating his creatures like puppets and imposing a preordained destiny upon them. After suffering a great trial, many people can no longer bear to hear the word 'God', since this unconscious projection prevents them from seeing in the many forms of violence that assail them, including accidents, the result of unfortunate human attitudes or choices, which should not be arbitrarily linked to the divine will. Suffering can blind us to the point where we can no longer see reliably or coherently. If human beings, whose love is limited, find such misfortunes so intolerable, how could a God, whose essence is the ultimate expression of love, not find them even more intolerable?[2] How could such a God not want for this or that woman more happiness in this life than even those who love them most here below wish for them, since his divine love corresponds, of its very nature with the highest manifestation of love anyone can be given?

When we stop being dependent on this projection of the human desire for omnipotence onto the representation of God, then we see how it has encouraged the tendency to confuse the freedom given to human beings with a permission to do evil. A certain kind of theological language thought it was right to use the formula: 'God does not want evil but he permits it.' Even though this is an advance on many approaches used in the past, this formula unfortunately fosters the incoherence it is trying to overcome: saying that God permits evil still gives the impression of relativising the horror of human suffering; and not only the horror of human suffering but also the horror of divine suffering, because a God of love must suffer cruelly from all the evil that is committed and be on the side of and at the side of all who suffer. Olivier Clément is one of the rare theologians to have been aware of the clumsiness of a language that refers to a divine permission to do evil: 'We must say that God has not created evil and also that he does not permit it.'[a] It is hard to grasp this insight at first, until we succeed in unmasking that mistaken correlation of human freedom with an indirect permission to commit evil. In fact, the correlation relies on the more or less unconscious supposition that this Creator-God could also have chosen from the start not to allow human beings their freedom. Indeed, it is only possible to 'permit' if you can oppose the project concerned and prevent it being carried out. A permission is not a permission if the one giving it was not in a position to forbid it. If we reflect on the link between the mystery of love and respect for the freedom of the one loved, it appears that a God, whose essence is love, has no choice between respecting human freedom or forbidding its exercise. Love cannot even contemplate depriving the loved one of his or her freedom, love is bound to respect the other's freedom, because all love can do is love! The fact that human beings can use their freedom badly does not mean a divine permission to commit evil of any kind. The existence of human

---

a   *Notre Père*, Paris, Socéval, 1988, p. 52.

freedom and respect for its exercise have to be inherent in the essence of a God of love, who would be unable to conceive – in word or deed – a relationship deprived of freedom. The existence of human freedom and respect for its exercise flows from the essence of a God of love, as water flows from a spring, because they alone correspond to a divine love that remains completely faithful to itself and could not do otherwise without denying its own nature.

A Limitless Love that Nothing can Quench

Little by little we discern a new face of divine omnipotence: an omnipotent love, which reveals its true identity in its capacity to love and go on loving whatever happens, whatever the rejections, disappointments and obstacles placed in its way. This new face is far removed from the most common representations of divine omnipotence. This distance between the two may even be so great that simply becoming aware of it, although absolutely necessary, may not on its own be enough to mitigate the impact of the unconscious projection of the infantile desire for omnipotence. The roots of such a psychological process lie so deep that intellectual awareness of its existence cannot on it is own destroy its hold. In so many books on the subject, we find a two-faced God. Their authors may not even realise it and may have accumulated an impressive theological or biblical baggage. It is as if this psychological process remained active in the subject, so that from time to time it reawakens a certain natural religiosity, which sits side by side with a more mature vision the authors thought they had acquired. Frequent reflection and regular renewal of this awareness are indispensable for anyone wishing to limit the influence of the projection of their own desire for omnipotence. Without a modicum of vigilance this project continues to mar from the outset any belief in a link between the mystery of God and the mystery of love and this will be proportional to the importance the religion in question accords to that link.

Any quest for meaning looking to Christian revelation needs to be even more vigilant in this respect, since recognition of a link between the mystery of God and the mystery of love lies at the heart of the gospel faith. As John the apostle expresses it with brilliant clarity: 'God is love.'[a] We cannot help misrepresenting the omnipotence of this God of love without regularly engaging in the discernment just described. Far from being like an infantile omnipotence with its secret aspiration to absolute, dictatorial control, the omnipotence of divine love cannot consist in forcing, manipulating or crushing human beings. It consists, rather, in the greatest respect for human freedom, continuing to accompany human beings whatever their lives are like, and loving them to the end, despite everything. Although it has inevitably been disfigured throughout history, it is this unknown face of divine omnipotence that is overwhelmingly revealed in the founding event of Christian faith: Christ's passion followed by his resurrection. Here we find revealed a divine omnipotence inseparable from that misunderstood, scorned and humiliated love, that succeeds in forgiving those who reject and crucify him and loving them to the end. Here we find divine omnipotence henceforth connected with the symbol of the cross; the sign of the cross is not chosen to exalt suffering, but to exalt that limitless love, from which nobody is excluded and expresses the Christian's confidence that nothing can separate him – neither him nor those he loves – from this divine love. 'For I am convinced that neither death, nor life [...] nor things present nor things to come, nor anything else in all creation will be able to separate us from the love of God in Christ Jesus our Lord.'[b] Here we see definitively revealed the only divine omnipotence that can claim to correspond with a God of love: an omnipotence whose face bears the expression of a limitless love that nothing can quench, discourage or prevent from pouring itself out inexhaustibly – a confident and reassuring love that evil will not have the last word.

---

a   1 Jn 4:8 and 16.

b   Rom 8:38, 39.

Creation in Essential Stages

However, evil also manifests itself in this world in forms that cannot be linked to the wrong use of human freedom. So this is where it constitutes the strongest challenge to the existence of an omnipotent God of love. In fact, it is sometimes difficult to set the boundaries between the manifestations of evil linked to the use of human freedom and those that are not so linked, since certain human decisions also have an indirect impact on many disasters which are called 'natural'. There is irresponsible ecological management, inappropriate or unapplied safety measures, installations built in high-risk zones, often for financial reasons, investments that do not give priority to the improvement of living conditions or to medical research, diseases that are badly diagnosed or treated, insufficient information campaigns or those that are not given due attention, without forgetting the frequent psychic origin of many illnesses linked to harmful human behaviour going back to childhood, and other psychosomatic troubles inseparable from each personal history and so on. But it remains undeniable that many phenomena, which sometimes have dramatic consequences for humanity, cannot be linked to a wrong exercise of human freedom, especially when they have been an integral part of creation since long before the appearance of human beings. Some of them are even embedded in the dynamic of evolution that enabled humanity to appear, beginning with the phenomena that cause the most outrage, reproaches and doubts about a Creator-God: natural disasters, diseases and, finally, death.

The unconscious projection of the infantile desire for omnipotence is again to be found at the heart of this inner process, which, in the presence of a world lacerated by these devastating aspects of creation, leads people to doubt the existence of an omnipotent God of love or to reproach him for not having created a better world. The power of this projection has an important role whenever it leads people to represent unconsciously the creative acts of such a God as like waving a magic wand, which instantly produces the desired result. The principal consequence of this illusory representation of a divine omnipotence that can do whatever it likes – the infantile fantasy par excellence – lies in the difficulty of taking into account a very simple truth: all creation passes through multiple stages before reaching its final form. The history of the Universe and the development of life on Earth are the most telling illustration of this and the scientific observation most apt to overthrow any quasi-magical representation of the activity of a Creator-God. The influence of this magical conception of divine activity often prevents us from understanding that the scientific theory of evolution does not challenge the existence of a Creator-God, but the representation that so many believers and non-believers make for themselves of God's creative ways. There is a big difference between the way in which a Creator-God might have gone about it and the question of his existence! This difference not only justifies the fact that there is no legitimate opposition between science and faith, but it also illustrates the valuable support that scientific observation is able to give to any inner development. This support does not mean that science is able to pronounce upon spiritual matters. The description of how the real world functions insofar as this can be observed – the scientific province, par excellence – is one thing, the meaning that can be given to this real world – the religious province par excellence – is another. Neither does this support mean that the vocation of science is to favour this or that interpretation of the observed facts. With these scientific discoveries and observations there will always be a choice to be made between the absurdity of chance[3] and a divine project that gives meaning to life and confirms the universally apprehended grandeur of love. By the same token, this support reminds us that even if science is not able to pronounce upon the existence of God, it still has the immense merit of confronting each of us with observed reality, rather than illusory dreams or pointless and often improbable speculations. If there is a Creator, the stages of evolution are what he himself decided to follow and which he therefore judged essential to accomplish his plan. Careful and respectful attention to scientific observations can thus actively contribute to freeing each of us from reductionist representations we always risk making of a possible Creator-God's way of working. It can do even more, because certain findings presented by science not only challenge the representation of God derived from the unconscious projection of the infantile desire for omnipotence. It also invites us to change the way we look at what we usually consider to be horrible defects in creation, which are incompatible with the existence of an omnipotent God of love. This apparent incompatibility appears in a completely different light when we take into account two scientific findings of the utmost importance.

Complex Evolutionary Intertwinings

The first of these findings is the discovery that the Universe has a history and that this history has an internal coherence. In order to cross the main complexity thresholds necessary to the development of life, it has run through stages that, retrospectively, can be seen to have been indispensable to evolution. The history of humanity is seen to be inseparable from the history of the Universe as a whole, in that all the major stages of evolution that have taken place for the last 14 billion (thousand million) years have played a crucial part in the progressive appearance of many elements that constitute human beings. This is beautifully illustrated by the formation of atoms, from their diversification through cosmo-chemical reactions at the heart of stars, to their diffusion throughout the Universe – and one day on planet Earth – thanks to the final explosion of the stars that spread them.[4] Scientific observation has discovered the exceptional potential for creativity and fertility made possible by the precise value of fundamental forces and constants in the universe. It has established that the slightest difference in their level would not have allowed the existence of elements that were ultimately constitutive of human beings.[5] It has also determined the importance of crossing certain complexity thresholds when evolution sometimes looked as if it could no longer progress. It has brought out the necessity of each major stage of evolution in order to reach the incomparable sophistication of a living creature with a consciousness capable of learning to love.[6] All this led science to an undeniable conclusion: the appearance and evolution of the human species could not have happened in any environment, but uniquely in the one that possessed the numerous elements and properties without which it has been shown that humanity could not have come into being. Theologically, this shakes any speculation about a magical omnipotence capable of making anything happen at any time in any way at all. Getting over this first stage towards a more mature and realistic vision of the challenges facing any Creator-God means giving up those illusory dreams of a creation that some might have imagined as conforming better with the existence of a God of love.

A second scientific finding leads us even further. It is intimately connected with the fact that the countless intertwinings between these different stages of evolution are so subtle and complex that they sometimes indirectly involve the manifestation of phenomena that have always disturbed us. Our ever more sophisticated understanding of the main cogs in this machinery, vital to the functioning of numerous natural phenomena, has brought out this paradoxical truth: among the elements that are most indispensable to the progressive emergence of developed life we find those that foster the most violent phenomena, beginning with natural disasters and numerous particularly harmful diseases.[7] To different degrees and in a way specific to each of them, all these phenomena are caused by and have contributed to a multitude of interactions between elements that enabled life to cross thresholds crucial to its development. In other words, scientific observation of these countless evolutionary intertwinings has shown plainly that even the elements presenting the most dangerous phenomena for humanity have played a part, in some way, in the appearance of the human species. This truth, apparently so paradoxical, leads to a surprising conclusion: the non-existence of these potentially dangerous phenomena – so strongly desired by a humanity that sometimes dreams of a creation it would have regarded as more successful – would have meant the non-existence of the elements that made human life possible! Theologically, this second conclusion invalidates any speculation about a Creator-God who could have chosen between creating a world like the one in which humanity evolved and creating a similar world in which there was no risk of dangerous secondary effects for his creatures.[8] Getting over this second stage towards a more mature and realistic vision of the challenges facing any Creator-God means giving up this false alternative that often presents itself to human thinking that is too dependent on the projection of the infantile desire for omnipotence.

Giving up on Creating a Loving Consciousness?

Our double finding invites us to give up depending on an illusory alternative. Then it leads us to take into consideration an alternative that really takes into account the stages that are apparently necessary to the evolution of life, the complexity of their evolutionary intertwinings and the risks they present to any living organism. Furthermore, seeing a coherent alternative means that scientific clarity leads to theological clarity, because this alternative cannot rely on theological speculations incompatible with the project or nature of a Creator-God who is love.[9] So we must be careful to place at the heart of our search the most faithful criteria for the motivations of a God of love. One criterion that is particularly useful for discarding a number of incoherent hypotheses is contained in this simple deduction: if there had been another way to create a conscious being whose capacity for love would have been superior to the human one, then a God of love would have used that way and not the way we see here below. Of course, we cannot say that this Creator-God would necessarily have found it impossible to choose another form of evolution or a Universe with different properties that would not have led to the same conditions. But it seems undeniable that a God of love would never had led the creation of humanity through limited, sometimes dangerous and painful stages, if a less risky, more direct or more promising way had been practicable. A second criterion of theological coherence and lucidity needs to be brought out. For reciprocal divine–human love to become really possible, this creation project had to endow human beings with a sufficiently developed level of consciousness and power of loving. The necessary degree of development is beyond our human knowledge and remains mysterious. Is it possible that the way of creation we see here below is not only the most promising but perhaps the only one able to guarantee a high enough degree of consciousness and capacity for love? There is also a third criterion to take into consideration, one that also shares in the mystery beyond human understanding.[10] Since a God of love would not act in a dictatorial way, he was bound to give a degree of freedom or relative autonomy to many elements of his creation, in accordance with their own nature. So, as well as the challenges mentioned earlier, there is that of ensuring in human beings the development of a degree of freedom enabling mutual consent without which a divine–human loving union would not be genuine. Moreover, a God of love would also attribute degrees of freedom or relative autonomy to all living organisms and, as far as possible, to matter itself. These different degrees of freedom or relative autonomy partly explain the countless fruitful or fruitless gropings seen throughout evolution, collaborating in their own way with the continual creative exploration done by a God of love. Despite the numerous imperatives in terms of precision, synchronisation and other parameters apparently necessary to cross certain complexity thresholds, would not such a Creator-God have insisted on setting up this exceptional potential for creativity and fertility so that his creative ingenuity could explore the best way to produce a conscious being capable of learning to love?

Finally, for discernment that takes account both of the reality of facts, their complexity, even necessity, and motivations corresponding to divine love, the most appropriate hypothesis would be a Creator-God facing an alternative that is radical in a different way from that imagined by human beings under the influence of the infantile desire for omnipotence: going through stages with consequences such as we see now or giving up on creating a degree of consciousness and a capacity for love high enough for reciprocal divine–human love!

An Endless Reciprocal Love

When we understand the dilemma, we are able to complete an important stage towards a clearer perception of the immensity of what is at stake, the balances and challenges facing a Creator-God who is love. From a psychological point of view, this stage is more commendable because any attempt to mourn the passing of a Magician-God raises internal resistance whose final throes manifest themselves with an intensity proportional to the deep-rootedness of the unconscious desire for omnipotence. From a philosophical and theological point of view, this stage is particularly decisive because it upsets the idea that certain manifestations of evil are incompatible with the existence of an omnipotent God of love. That idea is founded on the partly unconscious representation of a Magician-God, capable of guiding such an evolution without any risk of undesirable secondary effects. The famous theologian and scientist, Pierre Teilhard de Chardin, was one of the first to have developed a new perspective caused by a growing understanding of the evolution of the Universe and life on Earth. He was imbued with this deep conviction: 'It is true that for this problem [of evil] a better perspective on our Universe is beginning to bring the beginnings of an answer.'[a] This viewpoint offers a way to understand and even become reconciled with the world as it is. It offers this reconciliation to all those who take seriously the importance of evolutionary stages, countless elements, properties and other parameters that have to be respected in order for

---

a   *Sur la souffrance*, Paris, Seuil, 1974, p. 118.

the world to be able to give birth to sufficiently conscious and loving life. It offers reconciliation to all those who see that what they hold most dear in life here below would never have existed without the elements that sometimes risk indirectly causing the most unpleasant phenomena. It offers reconciliation to all those who question the true motivations that might have led a God of love to prefer the existence of this world to its non-existence and who glimpse an even greater plan than that which is apparent within the limited parameters of their earthly life: the Creator's plan to create a loving consciousness to live one day with him in eternal reciprocal love.

Apart from these questions, observation of the major stages of evolution remains a precious indication in any quest for meaning that no longer wishes to remain imprisoned by a representation of God in thrall to the infantile desire for omnipotence. If there is an omnipotent God of love, the omnipotence of his divine love is not the same as a magical omnipotence born of illusory dreams. Rather, it is an energy of creative love in continual activity, which does not become discouraged either by the many obstacles and risks inherent in setting up this kind of evolution – risks that may even be aggravated by his creatures when they misuse their free will – or by the extreme complexity and precision required in terms of properties, constants, multiple synchronisations and ingenious adaptations for the sake of the progressive emergence of a consciousness capable of loving.[11] Meditating on this very concrete aspect of divine love, that is unshakeable in its determination to bring another conscious loving being, Pierre Teilhard de Chardin was bold enough to write: 'Love is the most universal, the most formidable and the most mysterious of cosmic energies [...] The most expressive and most profoundly true way of telling the story of universal Evolution would be to trace the Evolution of Love.'[a]

This representation of divine omnipotence at least has the merit of being both in keeping with observed facts and fully coherent with a God of love, who would have acted differently

---

a   *Sur l'Amour*, Paris, Seuil, pp. 7, 10.

had he thought it possible to lead more directly to a similar or better result. It shows again how taking care not to remain too dependent on the unconscious projection of our own desire for omnipotence gives each of us the chance to stop distorting any belief that establishes a link between the mystery of God and the mystery of love. In the Bible, where this link is primordial, the notion of omnipotence is expressed by the Greek word *pantocrator*, which really means 'he who holds everything', holds all history in his hands, that is to say, he who has the power and determination to lead his creation to its fulfilment. So it is not a question of some magical power, but of a will and capacity to fulfil the ultimate aim of evolution, which the apostle Paul describes thus: 'God chose us in Christ before the foundation of the world to be holy and blameless before him in love.' [a] For Christian revelation, the aim of all this evolution is to bring about a conscious being, whom this Creator-God can admit into his own dimension to live in love with him. That is why Christian revelation believes that creation will not really be fulfilled until each of us has been raised. Accordingly, only the resurrection – and not earthly life – fully reveals the true face of this creative project and retrospectively confers all its value on each of the stages that have made it possible, rather as the beauty of a picture cannot be perceived in all its brilliance until the painter has really finished it.[12] Thus each of us is invited to look towards that world and that project of a God of love who created it.

Whatever people believe, what has to be recognised is the coherence of this confidence in an omnipotent God of love, who wants to have an eternal relationship with the most beautiful fruit of his creation. Nothing would be more contradictory and absurd than to have set everything going over the course of 14 billion (thousand million) years for the sake of the emergence of a consciousness capable of learning to love, only to plunge it back into nothingness, as if it had never existed. This view of an eternal love relationship reinforces the two specific features of that new face of a divine omnipotence, partly freed from certain

a   Eph 1:4.

unconscious determinisms: a prodigious creative ingenuity and an unfailing determination.[13] Both these features are characteristic of a love that is ready to brave all obstacles not to let anything separate it from a loved one whose freedom is always infinitely respected. These features are specific to any genuine love. That means that all of us – believers or not – must be careful no longer to let our quest for meaning depend on an illusory psychological projection that unconsciously fosters a feeling of incompatibility that is not, in fact, justified. The way this world works and the hazards involved do not contradict the existence of a divine love, whose omnipotence is, from the outset, serving the creation of a conscious being capable of one day leading a life of reciprocal love with God that will have no end.

PART 2

Guilt Feeling and Secret Fears of God

Unconscious Projections and Representations of Divine Judgment

Among the unconscious projections harmful to any spiritual quest, the most damaging are perhaps those that lead human beings to represent God – in whose existence they may or may not believe – as the Being who might judge them harshly, punish and even reject them. This second part of the book will unmask the true origins of such projections and thus enable us to free ourselves progressively from these secret fears. Those fears are inseparable from a real difficulty in believing ourselves worthy of being loved, and often lead to a repression of the God question or to an inner life that is more stymied than blossoming. Gradually, it will reveal a representation of divine judgment that is far removed from what human beings often imagine, following a difficult self-confrontation, especially when they are overcome by a more or less diffuse sense of guilt

A Difficult Self-Confrontation

Unmasking the true identity and origin of these unconscious projections means, first of all, recognising the fact that all human beings are beset by fears. These can extend from the simple fear of being disappointed or misunderstood to the fear of being unloved or even abandoned. However, these fears are not always clearly identifiable or conscious. Some of them lie deep in the human psyche in the most covert and subtle guise. Sometimes, they are even totally unconscious but still sufficiently present in each of us to influence our way of conceiving how God might see us. These fears may lead some to maintain a would-be religious indifference, to keep their distance, giving reasons that often look more like pretexts than the fruit of mature reflection. These same fears may lead others towards a spirituality that is entirely dependent on a multitude of conditions to be fulfilled, without which they believe they cannot be loved by God. This may mean that their inner life, or indeed their whole life, becomes like a prison governed by prohibitions, which may also affect their nearest and dearest. For both these groups, the flowering of an authentic quest for meaning or a spiritual quest must involve a clear understanding of this unconscious process.

Contrary to a fairly widespread opinion, these various secret fears of God not only develop from contact with a clumsy or too strict religious or parental education. Certainly, many fears are reinforced by teaching that has instilled the image of a strict God, by a strict parental upbringing, whose influence is all the stronger because the most common psychological transference in the representation of God is precisely that of the parent image. Moreover, every child has a tendency to assimilate subjectively a certain kind of educational language: 'If you behave well you will be rewarded, but if you behave badly you will be punished.' This becomes a kind of emotional blackmail, as if the parents' love for the child is in question. That often reinforces the impression that even a God of love will not love him or her if he or she does not first fulfil certain conditions. All these elements undeniably have repercussions on spontaneous representations of God, which beset many people who may call themselves 'believers' or 'non-believers'. It is nevertheless the case that the true source of these secret fears of being unloved, judged severely, punished, even rejected, lies at a much deeper level than the area of influence upon which education or possible external pressures might operate. The source is in fact inseparable from a stage that is inherent in the psychological development of every human being without exception. This stage sees certain unconscious data rise to the level of consciousness and confront each person with their inner darkness, aggressive drives, aspects of their history and personality which they dislike, that worry or disturb them to the point of causing such inner uneasiness. This delicate self-confrontation creates the difficulty of believing we are worthy to be loved – and therefore letting ourselves be loved. It drives us to represent God as the Being who might judge us severely because of aspects of our personality with which we have not yet succeeded in coming to terms. For each of us the risk remains high of unconsciously projecting onto God the severity with which we regard ourselves. This personal severity is sometimes just as unconscious as the projection to which it gives rise, since it is indeed true that only the unconscious has full access to certain hidden aspects of ourselves, which are sometimes harshly repressed. In other words, however clearly people see the severity with which they regard what they do not like about their own personality, part of themselves is beset by inner uneasiness that is inseparable from a sense of guilt.

Such inner uneasiness actively fosters the unconscious projection of that personal severity onto God. It can lead both those who are asking about God and those who are already leading an inner life in the wrong direction. Within both these groups, their representation of God risks remaining dependent on the real difficulty of believing ourselves worthy of being loved. Moreover, when the weight of this difficult self-confrontation, this sense of guilt buried very deep in each of us, is not taken into account enough in a certain theological language, then what might have been understood as 'good news' sometimes comes to be perceived as bad news![14] It is not accidental when in the middle of a theological reflection or Bible reading evoking particularly beautiful realities, a single slightly ambivalent expression, giving rise, for example, to any sort of ambiguity about divine love, that it is precisely this formulation that holds the attention and causes inner disturbance. It probably would not have found that resonance without the buried presence of an inner uneasiness fostered by this more or less unconscious sense of guilt.

Once this influence has been discovered, the question arises: how can we free ourselves gradually from this projection of the severity of our own view of ourselves unto God's view of us? That psychological process is deep-rooted in our being and always lurking for the slightest opportunity to grab us. Unfortunately, realising its influence is only the first step along the road. It is less a question of hoping to free ourselves finally from this projection than being continually alert to escape its hold upon us. Of course, this first stage is necessary to begin the task of limiting the projection's influence, because it enables us to recognise the part it plays in any harsh representation of God and therefore rightly to challenge its correctness. That creates an inner space where it becomes possible to envisage a new representation of God, which is not prey, from the outset, to this unconscious disfigurement. However, a second and even a third stage are equally necessary that enable us to reform our view of ourselves and the view of us we attribute to God. That is because they enable us to come into contact with and listen respectfully to the specific contribution of psychology and the no less specific contribution of Christian revelation. Fundamentally, the second stage consists in a better understanding of the various origins of the sense of guilt at the heart of each person's psychological development. That better understanding enables us to get rid of many judgments about ourselves and representations of God that are both illusory and damaging to any inner progress. As for the third stage, it is an attempt to discern more objectively how a Creator-God would view what a human being might dislike about him or herself. That attempt would try to get rid of unwarranted guilt and begin the healing of a certain kind of justified guilt feeling, while taking the first steps towards genuine self-reconciliation.

Origins of the Feeling of Guilt

During this second stage, in order to discern the various origins of the sense of guilt, we have to look as a whole – even if schematically – at the main stages of human psychological development during the first four years of life. One of the major contributions of psychoanalysis is to have shown that a sense of guilt is deeply rooted in each of us from infancy. It distinguishes this sense of guilt from that to which we commonly refer when speaking about remorse for having committed such and such an act that we judge – rightly or wrongly – to be reprehensible. The latter kind of guilt feeling will be discussed further on. But first we look at the emergence of a sense of guilt, which is all the more formidable because it leaves its mark upon the depths of the psyche from earliest infancy, even though it remains theoretically little known.

Psychology considers the emergence of a sense of guilt in early infancy as the result of the development of aggressive drives in the child. These aggressive drives can reach such terrifying proportions in the childish imagination that the child unconsciously feels guilty for harbouring such fantasies of destruction, hatred and even murder. For Melanie Klein, pioneer of child psychoanalysis in the 1920s, this surprising finding left no room for doubt: 'I know from experience how difficult it is to admit that these revolting ideas correspond to the reality, but analysis of very young children admits of no doubt. They offer precise evidence of the imaginary cruelties that accompany these ideas in all their abundance, strength and multiplicity.'[a] But how can these aggressive drives arise and then develop in this way in human beings?

The emergence of life is already a battle against nothingness and death. That means that every living being has to have a basic minimum of aggression in order to survive. Sigmund Freud notes the permanent struggle from birth onwards to escape from nothingness, a struggle that takes place in the depths of each being between a drive for life, which he calls 'Eros', and drive for death, which he calls 'Thanatos'. The psychoanalyst Jean-Pierre Chartier describes this first manifestation of aggression in these terms: 'Aggression then appears as the expulsion outwards of a destructive force originally directed against the subject himself.'[b] This potential for aggression follows a spectacular development over the course of the earliest years as a result of three major events, which have strong repercussions on the sense of guilt felt by the child, and on his severity towards himself: weaning, the appearance of the Oedipus complex and the formation of what Sigmund Freud calls the 'superego'.

The weaning period marks the first stage in the development of aggressive drives in the child, as the baby now realises that the mother's breast is not part of himself, that he cannot dispose at will of his main source of pleasure and comfort. Henceforth the mother image becomes ambivalent, a source of both happiness and unhappiness, love and hatred. Melanie Klein does not hesitate to state: 'Then the baby is dominated by tendencies to destroy the very person who is the object of all his desires, and who is closely linked in his mind with everything he experiences, good and bad.'[c]

The appearance of the Oedipus complex is another threshold the child's aggression crosses. His growing desire to unite with the parent of the opposite sex and keep that parent for himself alone, arouses in his unconscious the desire to make the same-sex parent disappear, as he or she is seen as a rival. This aggression

---

a   *La psychanalyse des enfants*, Paris, PUF, 'Quadrige', 2004, p. 144.

b   *Introduction à la pensée freudienne*, Paris, Payot, 1993, p. 145.

c   *L'amour et la haine*, Paris, 2001, pp. 86–7.

ends up being directed also at the parent of the opposite sex, partly because of a simultaneous phenomenon of identification, admiration and complicity with the same-sex parent, who is also exclusively desired (this is called the 'negative' form of the Oedipus complex) and partly because of the actual impossibility of uniting with the parent of the opposite sex: 'The principal object of all sexual desires, her father for the little girl and his mother for the boy, arouses hatred and vengeance, because these desires are not satisfied.'[a] This is one of the reasons why Sigmund Freud stresses the indirect link between the intensity of sexual drives and of aggressive drives, which, as the child has to repress them, are turned against himself in a sense of guilt: 'The prevention of erotic satisfaction leads to aggression towards the person who prevents that satisfaction, and that aggression has to be repressed.'[b]

Thus extremely violent aggressive drives towards his own parents unconsciously take hold of the child,[15] and then become the source of guilt and severity towards himself, developed even more strongly when his 'superego' is formed. As Jean-Pierre Chartier explains: 'The superego [...] is an unconscious forbidder. Afraid of losing his parents' love, the child internalises familial restrictions, the moral judgments and demands of his environment [...] This modified ego functions as an internal judge, who sometimes judges very fiercely.'[c] If the severity of this superego depends on 'family restrictions' and 'moral judgments' that become internalised, it is accentuated, according to Sigmund Freud, by the very intensity of the subject's aggressive drives, the rigour of the superego being to some extent proportional to their destructive tendencies: 'The action exerted on the conscience by this renunciation [of aggression] is such that all the aggression we abstain from satisfying is taken up by the superego and accentuates its own aggression against the ego.'[d] This severity of the superego

---

a   Ibid, p. 94.

b   *Malaise dans la civilisation*, Paris, PUF, 1971, p. 98.

c   *Introduction à la pensée freudienne*, op. cit., p. 141.

d   *Malaise de la civilisation*, op. cit., p. 86.

affects all children and not just those who have had to internalise a particularly strict parental education. On the one hand, in the course of his development every child has aggressive drives that are largely independent of his environment. On the other hand, even gentleness in the parents can, paradoxically, contribute to this severity of the superego, because the child will feel guilty about such aggressive drives towards such kind parents: 'A father who is too weak and indulgent will lead the child to construct an excessively severe superego, because such a child, feeling the love he is given, will have no recourse but to turn his aggression inwards.'[a] And Sigmund Freud adds: '[Anguish in the face of the superego], given the impossibility of hiding forbidden desires from the Superego, pushes the subject to punish himself still further.'[b]

---

a   Ibid, p. 88.

b   Ibid, p. 84

Don't Confuse the Superego with God

This unconscious tangle concealing the roots of an inner uneasiness, together with a difficulty of loving ourselves, a reluctance to believe we are worthy of being loved, and a severity towards ourselves often projected unconsciously onto God, remains so firmly embedded in the psyche that traces of it persist throughout life. These traces are more apparent during adolescence, when the new threshold crossed in the development of sexuality reactivates the Oedipus complex and causes a re-arousal of aggressive drives, at the same time amplifying an inner uneasiness so characteristic of that period of life. Although less apparent in adulthood, nevertheless, these traces continue to exert their influence, even if, according to Melanie Klein, the superego is at its severest in early infancy. 'It is precisely the primitive superego that is particularly severe [...] I have also found that the demands and prohibitions of the superego are not less unconscious in the young child than in the adult.'[a] So here we clearly see one of the greatest dangers threatening the representation that each of us – believer or non-believer – spontaneously creates of God: unconsciously confusing the very mystery of God with the superego, that is, with an 'internalised judge who sometimes judges fiercely', which has arisen from the internalisation of parental prohibitions, the moral judgments of our environment and the intensity of our

---

a   *La psychanalyse des enfants*, op. cit., p. 153.

own aggressive drives. That is one of the major reasons why Sigmund Freud had a tendency to see religions as the illusory fruit of unconscious projections. We have to admit the correctness of his judgment when the representation of God is effectively confused with the superego. However, it is important not to make a mistake here. Is it not one of the great benefits of a better knowledge of the psyche, and hence of the specific contribution of psychology, to become progressively liberated from possible religious illusions, not as a facile pretext to give up any spiritual development, but to have the means to set out, if we so wish, on a more trustworthy quest for God? In fact, when we learn to take care not to remain entirely dependent on the ill effects of certain unconscious projections, we develop the capacity to challenge and change our spontaneous representations of God. Then it becomes possible for each of us to open up to many unexpected discoveries and to go forward along the road of an ever more authentic spiritual quest.

This second stage invites us no longer to model our representation of divine judgment on the severity of the superego, no longer allow ourselves to be influenced here by the sense of guilt and secret fears that haunt every psyche. However, it does not thereby reveal how this divine judgment might differ from human judgment. A third stage now becomes necessary: to try to see how a Creator-God would view what human beings dislike about themselves. This attempt leads us to pay attention to what psychology and Christian revelation can mutually contribute to the subject of the two principal forms of guilt that possess the human heart. We have described the first, more unconscious kind, that arises from the darkest aspect of the person beset by misunderstood drives. The second is more conscious and produces remorse after we have done some deed or other we judge to be reprehensible.

Looking Clearly and Kindly

At first these very precocious aggressive drives look revolting and frightening in the most fundamental stages of their internal development and in their repression by parents and the superego. And yet psychology has discerned in them elements that are not only positive and constructive but necessary to the subsequent flowering of a person's capacity to relate – and in particular, the capacity to love. Indeed, is it not that minimum quantity of aggression, present from the beginning of life that guarantees survival, both in the struggles against external dangers and in the inner struggle against the death drive, which constantly threatens to destroy us? Is it not the impetuous strength of the desire to continue tasting a certain form of pleasure and fulfilment when breastfeeding that will later support the capacity to seek out what gives pleasure to loved ones, as well as remaining secretly possessed by a quest for fulfilment which, in a way, will help us to live and to hope? Is it not the mother's refusal to give in to the child's yearning for fusion that will not allow him or her to regress inwardly, but increasingly to become a whole, separate person, a person called to discover, develop and express what it is in its deepest self, a person called one day to know a loving union, whose intensity will leave nothing to envy in the union of fusion, but which will operate as respected otherness? Is it not the intensity of the Oedipean aspiration to be united with the parent of the opposite sex, indirectly the cause of murderous desires towards the other parent, that reveals the presence of a strong yearning to be loved and to love, which will characterise what is finest in us as adults and make us capable, if we so desire, of putting love first in our lives? Is it not thanks to the opposite-sex parent's refusal to satisfy Oedipal desires, a refusal that causes so much repressed aggression, that we will become capable of experiencing truly reciprocal love with another person we meet one day? Finally, is it not the repression of aggressive drives, enforced by the superego, that as well as introducing the control necessary to a common life, enables us to develop, through the guilt that this repression arouses, a desire to repair this fantasy evil, thus contributing indirectly to the flowering of ours own capacity to be attentive to the happiness of those close to us? Melanie Klein stresses this constructive use of the most obscure facets of the human being: 'In the unconscious of the child and adult, as well as destructive drives, there is a deep desire for self-sacrifice in order to help and make it up to loved ones whom one has harmed or destroyed in fantasy. The need to make people happy is linked in the depths of the spirit to a strong feeling of responsibility and concern about them, which manifests itself in the form of genuine sympathy for others and an ability to understand them as they are.'[a] According to her, these aggressive drives also play a constructive part in many areas: 'Aggression and hatred (the latter mitigated and to some extent compensated for by the ability to love) are often used in constructive ways ('sublimated', as it is called). Indeed, there is no fruitful activity, that does not have in it, under one form or another, a certain dose of aggression.'[b]

This overall long-term vision involves a complete reversal of the spontaneous view of these various drives and the stages of psychological development that arouse them in each of us. Rather than having to be considered negatively and continuing to foster a kind of guilt that is in fact unjustified, these drives can be set in their rightful place, as elements and stages, without which the human being would not have the psychic means one day to become a person capable of conducting relationships that are as constructive and beneficial as possible.[16] What we have seen in

---

a   *L'amour et la haine*, op. cit., p. 96.

b   Ibid, p. 97.

the history of the Universe, from its origins until the appearance of human beings, is equally applicable to each human history. Whatever their limits and possible undesirable secondary effects, all the previously described stages are indispensable for the development of a being capable of learning to love.[17] So it becomes possible to look at them clearly and kindly and to feel grateful for what could not have existed without them.

'God is Greater than our Hearts'

If psychological findings about human functioning allow each of us to look at ourself clearly and kindly, they also give precious indications to anyone wanting to discern more objectively how a Creator-God might look at these constitutive stages and elements of the human psyche. For who would be best placed to have an overall view of these multiple stages and to know the true value of these various elements? Surely a God who created human beings by choosing to make them pass through precisely these stages? That is an objective reason – more reliable than any illusory unconscious projections – to have confidence in the fact that no one could be better placed than a Creator-God to look clearly and kindly at what drives human beings, partly unconsciously, to consider themselves unworthy of being loved. Biblical revelation is aware of this from its very first verses: 'God saw all that he had made: it was very good.'[a] And it is expressed very forcefully in the First Letter of the apostle John: 'It will reassure our hearts before him whenever our hearts condemn us; for God is greater than our hearts, and he knows everything.'[b] [18]

'He knows everything' means, among other things, that as Creator he knows not only all the valuable findings made by science today or that could be made in the future, to keep on

---

a   Gen 1:31.

b   1 Jn 3:19–20.

improving our understanding of how the human psyche functions, but he also understands the true reason for them, their ultimate meaning. That meaning, that reason, which represents the specific contribution of religion in interpreting the phenomena observed by science, throws light from a different, complementary angle on the reason for these aggressive and sexual drives that are at the root of the feeling of guilt. In the light of the Christian vision of history, according to which the goal of evolution as a whole is to bring about the emergence of a being capable of one day living with God in an eternal loving union, the reason for these drives and the surprising power with which they manifest themselves, look very different. When human beings are seen to have always been destined to an ultimate, absolute and unlimited loving union and their deepest depths to have been created in a way that corresponds to this, there is no longer any reason to be surprised by the intensity, at first sight so disconcerting or even shocking, with which the baby aspires first of all to total fusion with its mother's breast, or that with which the small child then aspires to a loving union with the parent of the opposite sex, or that with which this same child, finding it impossible to satisfy his or her aspirations, comes to be haunted by extremely aggressive, even murderous drives.[19] How could a Creator-God not look kindly on such intensity, when by his very divine nature, he alone knows the incomparable intensity of the eternal union to which he has destined his creature?

Discerning the Mystery of Inner Beauty

As well as looking kindly and clearly upon us, this Creator-God would not stop at appearances, but would discern in each human being traces of inner beauty, even when that beauty was buried deep under infantile or immature manifestations, which still disfigure love or do not allow it to attain its fullness. Because God himself placed in each of us a deep yearning to know fullness of love, the Creator-God would again be the one best placed to know that this inner beauty characterises the human being's true identity. In the eyes of those who also do not want to stop at appearances, the presence of this powerful yearning to know fullness of love becomes the sign that they are no longer in the presence just of simple functional, animal, organic or psychic drives, but also facing a mystery. Is it not this mystery that is felt – sometimes unconsciously – by those who have experienced the wonder of genuine love and can no longer reduce it simply to biological attraction or reproduction of an animal species to ensure its survival? That is how Christian mysticism perceived it, in whose eyes human love is like a reflection here below of divine love and eternal union, as the theologian Olivier Clément says: 'If the Song of Songs is a love song – of both erotic and affectionate love – which symbolises the union of God and the soul, that is because human love, of any kind, has something to do with God, and remains for many one of the only mystical experiences given to them here below [...] Many lives [...] understand, in the light of a theological exploration of the passion of love, that they have been devoted, perhaps by that very passion, to a quest for the Absolute. Truly spiritual people know and respect that.'[a] A Christian theology that focuses on the essential, that is attentive to what might support a particularly beautiful and intense union with God, remains aware that each human being experiences or will experience one day a reciprocal love with God, dependent on his or her confidence in being loved and capacity for loving. In the very intensity of erotic drives, it discerns one of the most beautiful means language has to express the intensity of love for a partner within a couple, to increase each person's confidence in being loved and capacity for loving.[20] That insight also leads to a new look at Sigmund Freud's almost obsessional insistence on questions of sexuality – an insistence often misunderstood since, behind it, there was probably a deeper intuition, perhaps of a mystical kind. That was the impression of Carl Gustav Jung, a psychoanalyst contemporary with Sigmund Freud: 'In sum, [Freud] wanted to teach – at least it seemed to me – that considered from the inside, sexuality also includes spirituality or possesses an intrinsic meaning. But his materialist terminology was too limited to be able to formulate this idea. So I had the impression of him that, basically, he was working towards finding his own goal and finding himself [...] Freud never asked himself why he had continually to be talking about sex, because this thought had so completely taken over him. He never realised that the "monotony of interpretation" betrayed a flight from himself or from that other part of himself which should perhaps be called "mystical". But without recognising that side of his personality it was impossible for him to be in harmony with himself [...] That is why I see in him a tragic figure, because he is a great man, and, what is more, he had the sacred fire.'[b] [21]

We have tried to discern more objectively how a Creator-God might look at the first origins of the sense of guilt, in its most unconscious form, which is the form most likely to foster in

---

a   *Corps de mort et de gloire*, Paris, Desclée de Brouwer, 1995, pp. 79, 84.

b   *Ma vie*, Paris, Gallimard, pp. 179–180.

human beings a difficulty in believing they are worthy of being loved. Now we must do the same for the most conscious and, therefore, best known sense of guilt, that which takes hold of us as a result of an action which we judge – rightly or wrongly – to be reprehensible. There too it is important to seek the specific contributions of psychology and Christian revelation.

A God who Knows Each One's Wounds

One of the most specific and fundamental tasks undertaken by psychology has always been to try to understand the human heart better, particularly what drove it to react in this or that way, to do this or that deed. This investigation is non-judgmental, but that is not to deny the reality of the evil committed – when it has been committed – or to relativise the gravity of that evil – when it is grave – but because the very nature of psychology's task is to focus essentially on this untiring attempt at understanding human depths. Among the findings it has come up with over time, there is one that throws important light on what leads a human being to react negatively: acts of aggression derive in one way or another, directly or indirectly, from wounds that are already present in their perpetrator. These wounds are not necessarily linked to the person towards whom the aggression is aimed. Neither are they necessarily recent or even conscious wounds, but their presence is strong enough to seek external expression from time to time in the most varied ways, which may be harmless or harmful.

If each of us had total clarity in this area, many of us would realise with astonishment the considerable impact of our personal wounds on our negative behaviour, which sometimes makes it hard for us to love ourselves. This would also reveal our tendency to represent God – whether we believe in him or not – as a Being inclined to judge harshly or punish us, because this tendency originates in the unconscious projection onto God of our own severity towards

ourselves. The only way to overcome our strong internal resistance
to letting ourselves be loved is to take into account the existence of
wounds, perhaps already known, or repressed at an age when they
could not be coped with and which have not yet become conscious,
or even wounds that may always remain unknown to us but whose
gravity, however mysterious, should not be underestimated. This
process is not an easy one. Such realism is more difficult than
letting ourselves slip down the slope of self-denigration which
becomes self-hatred. In its exploration of humanity's darker sides,
psychology has known for a long time that it is much easier for a
troubled spirit to sink into self-destruction, to go along with its
death drive – and paradoxically end up enjoying it – than to learn
to love itself and be loved. True courage is not always found where
many people think it lies. There was a reason why Sigmund Freud
called that destructive drive 'Thanatos', always on the lookout for
what it can use to drag the human spirit down, to sap its life force,
in particular, by damaging the self-image and image it has of others.
If we make the effort to take into account the wounds that are the
source of such and such an action or thought, this helps us see
the truth about ourselves. That truth is deeper than a subjectivity
blinded by appearances has any inkling of. It also leads us to look
with the same discernment at our fellow humans, and come to see
behind many actions that at first seem negative – in them and in
ourselves – wounds that need healing. They are crying out to be
better understood, recognised and loved.[22]

If all these inner wounds, large or small, are linked, in one
way or another, to this hurt at – rightly or wrongly – not feeling
well enough understood, recognised and loved, how could a God
who created human beings, and hence would be better placed
than anyone to understand their functioning, himself fall into the
trap of appearances and not perceive the perpetrator's hidden
suffering behind all the evil committed? How could he fail to
know that evil does not mean that the depths of the human
being in question are evil in themselves, but that they are fundamentally wounded? So the powerful statement of one who may
have been Christ's closest confidant during his earthly life has an
even stronger resonance: 'It will reassure our hearts before him

whenever our hearts condemn us; for God is greater than our hearts, and he knows everything.'[a]

'He knows everything' means, of course, that he knows all the wounds suffered by each of us, including wounds formerly repressed, which have not yet reached consciousness and even those that never do throughout a lifetime. But it also means that he knows about a wound that is both more mysterious and even deeper, a wound that by its very nature escapes all scientific investigation, because only the ultimate meaning of human existence, and no simple observation of how it functions, reveals its presence and enables us not to underestimate its impact on every heart. Since, as Christian revelation holds, human beings are created one day to live a life of eternal loving union and, since they aspire to this in premonitory fashion from the beginning of their lives, how could they not suffer from the wound inflicted by the huge gap between that infinite love, to which we are destined, and the love we experience here below? That wound affects every human being without exception, because even the most wonderful love some people may experience during this earthly life cannot be compared with that divine love, for which our deepest self has been created. Once again, who is capable of measuring the extent of this wound and taking it into account, better than a Creator-God, who would have full knowledge of the true intensity of that eternal love and therefore of the felt lack of it – conscious or not – by each human being? This lack, which leads the author of the Letter to the Hebrews to write that human beings are 'strangers on Earth'[b] and that longing which leads St Augustine to say that the human heart is 'restless until it rests in [God]'[c] are the source of a wound inherent in the human condition. It is hard to imagine that this ontological wound is not also taken into account by God when he looks at what human beings dislike about themselves, or various aspects of a person with whom they are not yet reconciled.

a   1 Jn 3:19–20.

b   Heb 11:13–16.

c   Confessions 1:1.

A Love from which No One is Excluded

When we perceive God's ability to see evil as the consequence of various secret wounds of the human heart, this enables us to form a completely different representation of divine judgment, which a mature Christian faith sees in the overwhelming characteristic care shown by Christ never to exclude anyone from his love. The fundamental viewpoint of this judgment is not to seek to condemn human beings, but to keep trying to cure the inner wounds, without which their inclination to do evil could not have developed in the way it has. This should not be confused with a disregard of evil or a relativisation of the gravity of evil, those two aspects so often attached to the Christian idea of forgiveness. Indeed, not only does this care to bring about inner healing exclude, by its very existence, any disregard of evil, but it also shows how seriously that evil is taken. Rather than denying or relativising the seriousness of the evil committed, this divine forgiveness is the highest manifestation of a continual struggle to eradicate evil by attacking its true root, by treating it where it lies in the human heart, that is, by healing the wounds there instead of making them bigger by a superficial judgment.[23]

'Christ's death on the cross is a judgment of judgment' wrote Maximus the Confessor in the seventh century.[a] He realised that Christ's attitude in his Passion reveals, above all, a God who,

---

a Questions à Thalassius, 43 (PG 90, 408) quoted and translated by Olivier Clément in *Sources, les mystiques chrétiens des origines*, Paris, Stock, 1992, p. 47.

even when abandoned, judged and condemned, does not himself abandon, judge or condemn anyone, but continues to love until the end, and even to love those who crucify him.[a] Thus the cross has become the Christian symbol par excellence, not to connive with a view of life that glorifies suffering, but because, at that particularly dramatic moment, Christ brought the revelation of a passionate love to its highest degree of intensity. It is love that was without limits and offered to all without exception. It is a passionate love that sums up, confirms and explains all the actions undertaken by Christ in the course of his life; a passionate love that gives a remarkable criterion for meditating on his words and freeing them from interpretations contradicting his deeds – interpretations often produced mistakenly by the unconscious activity of the lurking sense of guilt, on the lookout for the least ambiguity to be exploited.[24] It is a passionate love that calls upon us not to remain imprisoned by our unconscious projection onto God of a severity towards ourselves and the various secret fears this constantly fosters, but to challenge, set aside or redefine these representations of the divine attitude that are inconsistent with such a love.[25] Among the latter, popular representations of hell deserve special treatment, since they are symptomatic of the omnipresence in human beings of this sense of guilt, this unconscious projection onto God of our own harsh view of ourselves, this real difficulty in believing we are worthy to be loved. Freeing ourselves progressively from the influence of such a projection enables us to come to the only interpretation of hell that is fully compatible with the judgment of a God of love: not the condemnation of a human being, but, as Olivier Clément says, the possibility left to that human being freely to refuse or to accept the divine love that is always being offered: 'So this love can be refused by a person who shuts himself off and withdraws into himself, [...] for the human being has this final freedom, and then that is the mystery called "hell". [...] I remember meeting a great contemporary mystic, Father Sofrony, from Mount Athos. When I asked him what would happened if a human being

---

a   'Father, forgive them, they don't know what they are doing', Lk 23:34.

refused to open his heart and to welcome this love offered to him, he replied: "Be sure that, as long as there is anyone in hell, Christ will be with him." […] God remains at the gateway to every heart, even hearts that are closed to him, and if necessary, he will wait for all eternity for these hearts to open to him."[a]

Thus, little by little, we see revealed the imperfectly known face of divine judgment that is quite different from what we so often imagine when in the grip of a largely unconscious sense of guilt. That sense of guilt has an equally unconscious tendency to confuse the mystery of God with the superego, with a view of itself whose severity may be projected onto God. In fact, it betrays a poor self-understanding, particularly of the part played by our own inner wounds in doing some deed or other we judge to be reprehensible. Becoming aware of this powerful influence, moving towards a better understanding of the principal stages of our own psychological development – with its drives, frustrations and wounds – seeing God as looking clearly and kindly upon us, gives us the means to glimpse a divine judgment that only seeks to heal the deepest wounds of the human heart, free it from its secret fears. It seeks to give us newer levels of confidence in being loved and in our power of loving, and to bring every human being into a reciprocal love that exceeds our wildest hopes.

---

a   *Taizé, un sens de la vie*, Paris, Bayard-Centurion, 1997, pp. 98, 101.

PART 3

From Distant Condescension to Reciprocal Love

Unconscious Projections and Representations of Divine Transcendence

A Being who is distant, domineering or condescending. Such spontaneous representations of God probably contribute most to fostering a certain religious indifference or spiritual luke-warmness. They make some people feel no particular interest in the question or God. They sometimes lead others to confine their faith either within a narrow moralistic frame, to the detriment of their spiritual lives, or to a spirituality mostly reduced to a pious master–slave relationship. These representations of God derive mainly from unconscious psychological projections, manifested when God is seen as a transcendent Being, a divine transcendence, to which these projections tend to ascribe a domineering and distant grandeur. The unconscious aspiration to such grandeur lies in the depths of every human being, believer or non-believer and risks being projected regularly onto their representation of God. This third part of the book aims to unmask the influence of this psychological projection and to discern the characteristics of a divine grandeur that are really compatible with a God who is love. This will reveal a completely different representation of divine transcendence, no longer synonymous with distant condescension but with possible closeness and even reciprocal divine–human love.

We attempt to identify and set aside the main psychological determinisms, which often prevent us reconciling our representation of divine transcendence with the possibility of a reciprocal divine–human love. This reflection will have to confront obstacles of a theological, philosophical and psychological nature, which prevent our reconciling this divine transcendence with the presence in God himself of a desire to be loved – a divine desire without which no reciprocal love could exist. When we think about the possible existence of this divine desire, we will begin to question and even overturn many ways of apprehending God or leading an inner life. It will invite each of us to change the way we think about our own capacity to love. In the course of our journey, we will show and deepen the true foundations for confidence in the fulfilment of this reciprocal divine–human love, to which many mystical traditions have tirelessly borne witness throughout the ages. These foundations will be shown in a new light by Christian revelation, for which such reciprocal love constitutes both the heart and the peak of any spiritual quest.

Freeing Ourselves from a Domineering God

There is a double difficulty in any attempt to clarify the unconscious projections linked to the secret aspiration to domineering grandeur that lurks in the depths of every human being. On the one hand, the concept of grandeur spontaneously represents a positive reality, which does not lead us to beware of its possible negative repercussions on our inner life. On the other, many believers would feel they were lacking in respect, even blaspheming, if they dared to fall away from what God's greatness inspires in them. It is therefore important to make clear that the analysis of this psychological process does not question divine grandeur as such, but the way in which human beings are apt to conceive it.

Even before it becomes dependent on more developed unconscious projections, our representation of divine grandeur is subject to what psychology calls 'transference'. Unlike the projection of an attribute which the subject possesses himself, without consciously admitting it (for example, his own desire for omnipotence or the harshness of his own self-judgment), transference consists in projecting a relationship with another person or an attribute specific to another person known by the subject (for example, the relationship with his father or his father image) onto a representation of God. Applied to the greatness of a transcendent God, the most natural transference will be that of attributes linked, in one way or another, to what a human being identifies as a state of grandeur here below, that is, attributes commonly assigned to social, worldly, hierarchical, political etc. grandeur. That is why secular, scriptural or liturgical spiritual traditions have had a tendency to evoke God by multiplying references to 'Lord', to a 'celestial majesty', or other similar expressions. That transference, however understandable, inevitably fosters the impression that an eminently respectful distance should be the mark of any relationship with such a God. Indeed, a personal relationship will differ according to whether, consciously or not, we identify the other as a powerful figure in this world or an intimate, by whom we know we are loved. The way we behave, express and entrust ourselves, expect or offer love will be very different. This fact emphasises the considerable influence of the mental image attached to the idea of God. The importance of this image remains, even for those who are conscious that a mature faith consists, above all, in an intense interpersonal relationship with God, and not in abstract ideas of moralising principles. Therefore, this transference process requires a certain vigilance on the part of those who do not wish to see their spiritual journey go wrong from the beginning because of a too human representation of divine grandeur, especially if such a representation leads them, from the outset, to identify that divine grandeur with a grandeur that imposes itself.

To this relatively elementary transference, another, more subtle unconscious determinism is added. This is the projection of the desire for domineering grandeur that each of us carries in us from infancy. Its origins lie in infancy, because that is the period in which the child discovers himself to be very limited, and dislikes the experience. Countless frustrations end up creating permanently in the depths of his being a strong aspiration to a kind of grandeur inseparable from a certain power, a certain control, even a certain domination. That powerful, secret aspiration remains sufficiently deep-rooted to leave traces until adulthood and to regain its influence at any time when we feel the strain of the undeniable limits to which each of us is subject throughout life. Things we have to consent to or renounce are not the only things that regularly revive this aspiration towards grandeur.

Humiliations suffered within the family, among friends, at school or at work also reinforce it, even though it may remain unconscious. This aspiration to dominating grandeur may find in the religious sphere a perfect setting for projection, so that there is a real risk for each of us unconsciously to associate the idea of God with this domineering grandeur, which our unconscious wants to possess. That association has damaging consequences for a spiritual journey because it often confines the inner life to a dominant–dominated relationship, from which the very idea of a possible reciprocal relationship, worthy of the name, is excluded. The association may even cause a systematic spiritual blockage in people who have had to struggle in the past to free themselves from excessively harsh parental authority, from an authoritarianism that their infant eyes identified with a certain form of parental grandeur.

One of the major difficulties for any discernment seeking to become less dependent on this psychological process consists in the frequent cohabitation of this partly unconscious representation of God with a more conscious, often more mature, representation which imagines it has ousted the former and does not suspect that it still continues with its underground activity. That juxtaposition, whether occasional or continuous, may occur because the unconscious process is so deep-rooted and capable of popping up unexpectedly. Unmasking it is sometimes a delicate matter, because this cohabitation does not necessarily translate into theological convictions or propositions. More subtly, it manifests itself at moments within a context not bereft of hope or beauty, through attitudes, gestures and symbols that betray, unknown to the person concerned, the hold this unconscious representation of divine grandeur still has over him or her. Its most widespread manifestation is perhaps that expressed during a sermon or a Bible reading or, in a completely different context, in a theatrical, dramatic or satirical presentation, when the intonation of the human voice imagines it is reproducing the divine voice by suddenly becoming firm, strict, almost tyrannical. This process takes many other forms, among which we may list peremptory statements in theological language presenting a two-faced God, the pronunciation of uncompromising judgments uttered in God's name, the authoritarian gestures of a preacher, the heaviness of certain religious rituals, the excessive ornamentation of liturgical vestments etc. If such manifestations are sometimes motivated by a sincere desire to pay homage to divine grandeur, the question still needs to be asked: in honour of what divine grandeur? That of a king surrounded by his obedient and servile court? That of a dictator worshipped by a mob that is really afraid? In any case, it is difficult to perceive the grandeur of a God whose mystery is closely linked to the mystery of love. It is useful, even essential, to question the nature of this divine grandeur in any search for meaning in a belief where the link between the mystery of God and the mystery of love is pre-eminent. The closer the link, the more likely it is that the belief will be disfigured by the unconscious determinisms we have just unmasked.

For Christian revelation where the very essence of the divine mystery is held to correspond to the ultimate expression of love, vigilance is even more important because the distance is so great between the height of such divine love and the depth of the unconscious projection of a human thirst for domineering grandeur. That distance demands a crucial inner reversal to discern the true nature of the grandeur of a God whose very essence is love. The belief is not in just any divine grandeur, but the grandeur or greatness of divine love. So what characterises great love but its quality, the quality of love offered to the loved one? Christ himself tries to make his disciples aware of this necessary change of perspective by inviting them several times no longer to identify divine grandeur or any other form of true grandeur with a grandeur that is domineering, crushing, dominating. His teaching and behaviour are witness to it: 'For who is greater, the one who is at the table or the one who serves? Is it not the one at the table? But I am among you as one who serves.'[a] Highly symbolic actions illustrate the point in unexpected ways, for example, his messianic entry into Jerusalem in the course of which 'Jesus found

---

a Lk 22:27.

a young donkey and sat on it'[a] or in the washing of feet, which the apostle John presents as a manifestation of the greatness of divine love by saying at the beginning of the story: 'Having loved his own who were in the world, he [Jesus] loved them to the end.'[b] Lastly, the gift of his life on the cross transforms what a human being would think of as a tremendous humiliation[c] into a startling manifestation of love: 'No one has greater love than this, to lay down one's life for one's friends.'[d] These are calls to realise that true greatness lies in the quality of a person's love. And it seems legitimate to expect the highest manifestation of it from a God who is both the source and the ultimate expression of love. But it also allows us to glimpse the extent of the inner conversion required to move from the representation of a domineering divine grandeur to that of a divine greatness synonymous with a great love that keeps on revealing itself to be even greater.

---

a   Jn 12:14.

b   Jn 13:1.

c   'He humbled himself and became obedient to the point – even death on a cross', Phil. 2:8.

d   Jn 15:13.

Freeing Ourselves from a Distant God

There is another secret aspiration, just as ancient as the thirst for domineering grandeur and buried just as deep in the human psyche. It too is unconsciously projected onto the spontaneous representation of divine transcendence. This is the desire to gain and enjoy completely self-sufficient autonomy. Under the influence of such a projection, the representation of divine transcendence may be perceived as a distant grandeur so self-sufficient that it is not at all concerned to seek any closeness of reciprocal relationship. This strong aspiration towards a distant autonomy is active in each of us and should not be underestimated, since the progressive acquisition of a certain autonomy sums up a great many of the efforts made throughout the first years of life. In many respects, gaining this autonomy is an incessant struggle, in the course of which the physical and mental limitations of the infant regularly make inroads into his self-image. These limitations inflict a narcissistic wound, fostered by the permanent need to ask others to do things he cannot yet do himself, an absolute dependence on parental figures, whose apparent omnipotence the child envies. Moreover, this narcissistic wound, inherent in every child, is often made worse by certain kind of adult behaviour, which, as the child psychoanalyst Francoise Dolto says, humiliates the child when they do not respect him or her as 'an autonomous person in the making'[a]

---

a *Les chemins de l'education*, Paris, Gallimard, 1994, p. 96.

in 'everyone's vocation to become a free man or woman.'[a] All these elements are highly likely to foster in the unconscious a confusion between a state of grandeur linked to personal accomplishment and a state of self-sufficiency whose highest manifestation would be not only not to turn to anyone for help but also, in thrall to reactionary narcissism, no longer to want to create too strong links with anyone at all.'[26]

How can we not suspect the impact of that confusion on the unconscious representation of a divine Being, whose nature is rightly thought to correspond to the highest and fullest state of grandeur there is? Many spiritualities conceal within them a form of distant divine grandeur. Their theological expressions are spontaneously accepted, all the more easily because they correspond with this unconscious aspiration in each of us. The process partly explains why we fail to mistrust various versions of this distant, even impassive God, who is content to sit throned in authority and does not have any aspirations to relate to others. Such theological speculations seem so much a matter of course that it becomes hard seriously to challenge the illusory conditioning that they impose. However, these representations should not be trusted so readily. They seem to be fostered by a reaction of pride to the narcissistic wound each of us receives when coming to terms with our inherent limitations.

If we take a cool look at these spontaneous representations of divine transcendence, we will question the trustworthiness of their original foundation, that is, the unconscious confusion between a state of grandeur linked to personal accomplishment and a state of self-sufficiency that tries to keep its distance. In its search for a better understanding of the human psyche and relationships, psychology has found something else about what characterises a state of accomplishment, maturity and fulfilment in human beings. We grow and really blossom when our various inner prisons no longer prevent us from leading interpersonal relationships that are as harmonious as possible. That is why one of the principal aims

---

a   Ibid, p. 154.

of various psychotherapies and psychoanalyses is to contribute as much as possible to dismantling this or that block sometimes stopping us from having full access to our capacity to establish well-chosen and constructive interpersonal relationships. Rather than corresponding to a state of withdrawal, a healthy autonomy is thought to support human fulfilment and growth by enabling us to build chosen, positive relationships, and for some of us these will culminate in married, parental or fraternal love. This reverses the representation of divine transcendence corresponding to the fullest and most perfect state of grandeur possible. The grandeur and perfection of divine transcendence are closer to the ultimate expression of the desire and real capacity to lead flourishing and constructive interpersonal relationships. The more faith recognises the link between the mystery of God and the mystery of love, the more the grandeur of divine transcendence will be linked to such a God's capacity and desire to lead loving relationships with human beings, and not to keep himself at a distance in cold self-sufficiency.

This shows the extent of the change of perspective required to represent the transcendence of a God whose nature is closely related to love. Our faith is not in any transcendence but in the transcendence of divine love. So what would characterise transcendent love better than the capacity and desire to overcome all the obstacles that might keep it away from the loved one? What is more foreign to the logic of love than an attitude that keeps a haughty distance from the loved one? The Christian mystery of the Incarnation, of a God who comes to share our earthly life for love's sake, poignantly illustrates this change of viewpoint, which is one of the most astonishing features of Christian spirituality. Unlike many other kinds, Christian spirituality does not stress a multitude of conditions to be fulfilled or ascetic efforts to be made in order to be united to God, a reality or ultimate state that is almost inaccessible here below. On the contrary, it reverses that tendency and relies fundamentally on the love of God who wants to be united with each of us even in our human conditions, there where we are, in order to invite us to enter now into a reciprocity of love with him.[a] This is a puzzling and incomprehensible mystery if our representation of divine transcendence is still unconsciously associated with a haughty and distant grandeur, but an overwhelming and meaningful mystery if it is viewed in terms of the internal logic of love, which wants only to be united with the loved one. The transcendence of a God of love should not be represented as a distant self-sufficiency but as a love that is willing to overcome the most apparently insurmountable obstacles. That is another reason to represent a divine Being who ardently desires to be with human beings, and invites them to enter into a relationship with himself where closeness[b] and reciprocity[c] are both given their rightful place in any love that is worthy of the name.

The conditioning inherent in various projections of a desire for dominant or distant grandeur is not the only kind that make it difficult to represent a divine transcendence that wishes to engage in a reciprocal divine–human love. Reciprocal love implies the existence in both parties concerned not only of a desire to love but also of a desire to be loved. Various kinds of inner resistance may make it particularly difficult to recognise a desire, in God himself, to be loved by human beings. Such a recognition comes up against major blocks, of a theological, philosophical and psychological kind. These must be removed one by one. The first block comes from the tendency, fostered by a certain natural religiosity, to see in God only the Being who can satisfy all kinds of human need, so that the fact that he himself might also have expectations is neither suspected nor taken into account. The

---

a   'I made your name known to them, and I will make it known, so that the love with which you have loved me may be in them, and I in them.' According to the Gospel of John the apostle, these were the words Christ spoke to God before his Passion (Jn 17:26).

b   'And remember, I am with you always, to the end of the age' (Mt 28:20). 'I will not leave you orphaned [...] I will ask the Father and he will give you another Comforter to be with you for ever. This is the Spirit of truth' (Jn 14:18 and 16).

c   'As the Father has loved me, so I have loved you; abide in my love [...] Abide in me as I abide in you' (Jn 15:9 and 4).

second block comes from the tendency, fostered by a certain type of theological reflection, to insist almost exclusively on the sacrificial and disinterested nature of divine love – a stress that is probably linked to the influence of a philosophical inheritance that has long been concerned to exclude any need, lack or desire from the Deity. The third block comes from the tendency, fostered by a certain evangelical Christian theology, to fear that recognising any desire to be loved in God himself might make the satisfaction of that divine desire a condition to be fulfilled in order to be loved by God – a condition which contradicts Christ's new message that the gift of divine love is gratuitous and unconditional. The fourth block comes from the tendency, fostered by a lack of self-esteem, not to believe in the hidden beauty of our own capacity to love, to the point where we do not even suspect that a God of love might appreciate that hidden beauty and want to be loved himself by each of us.

Reciprocal Love for its Own Sake

The first block is typical of a certain natural religiosity that is omnipresent since the beginning of the history of human spirituality. That religiosity could be summed up as the attempt to coax or soften up the divinity through rituals, services, sacrifices, prayers, with a view to obtaining a return, such as advantages, the granting of a request, power, success etc. We cannot help but see that such an attitude is more like a kind of bargaining or blackmail, albeit only emotional blackmail, than like a truly mature reciprocal relationship.[27] Sigmund Freud thought he had discovered the psychic origin of this attitude in the unconscious desire in the grown-up adult human to continue, through their belief in a Father-God, to have a parental figure who could protect them and supply their needs when asked. According to Freud, this is a 'father nostalgia', whose development coincides with the inevitable realisation, some day or other, that there are inherent limits in parents' capacity to respond to the needs and anguish of the grown-up child. 'As for religious needs, attachment to the infantile state of absolute dependence, as well as nostalgia for the father that this state arouses, seems irrefutable. It is even more so because that feeling is not only caused by a survival of infantile needs, but it endures because of the anguish humans feel at the powerful predominance of fate.'[a]

---

a   *Malaise de la civilisation*, op. cit., pp. 15–16.

However that may be, it seems undeniable that many behaviours that are called 'religious' or 'pious' betray more self-concern than any real concern for God. When only the expectations of the human being in question are taken into account, he or she is so self-preoccupied that the spontaneous representation of God leaves no room for a possible desire in God himself to be loved. In these circumstances, what God might feel or expect is simply not thought of, left out of the picture. God may be the one most prayed to but he is also the most forgotten, as Olivier Clément stresses: 'The one who is the most excluded, the one who is the most forgotten, the one who is most often misunderstood, is God.'[a] Indeed, with this natural religiosity, partly fostered by 'father nostalgia', God can only be the giver, the one who is there to satisfy human demands. Otherwise, 'what's the point in believing?' – a question whose logic is more commercial than spiritual.[28] This powerful conditioning of the representation of God illustrates once more the impact of the unconscious on a form of natural religiosity, which, even if it does not go to the excesses that some have called 'illusions', often prevents us from glimpsing other perspectives, from conceiving or living spiritual experience differently.

Such conditioning also illustrates the extent of the change of heart to which we are called by any belief in a God whose mystery is intrinsically linked to love. As for Christian spirituality, it sees maturity of faith as the flowering of an inner life in which the believer loves God for his own sake and not in order to get anything from him. It is a question of loving him for the sake of loving him, loving for love's sake, since the goal of true love is love itself. In Christ's eyes, nothing is higher than such a love, which involves the whole being: 'You shall love the Lord your God with all your heart, and with all your soul, and with all your mind.'[b] One of Francis of Assisi's dearest wishes was to be attentive to God for his own sake, to enter into reciprocal love for its own sake, learn to taste the beauty of that reciprocity, come

---

a   *Taizé, un sens de la vie*, op. cit., 1997, p. 77.

b   Mt 22:37.

what may, whatever went on in his own life with its fluctuations and burden of cares. According to the words attributed to him by the Franciscan Eloi Leclerc: 'God is, that is enough, murmured Francis [...] To discover that God is God, eternally God, beyond what we are or might be, rejoice wholly in what he is [...] to thank him for himself, for his unfailing mercy, that is what this love demands at its deepest.'[a] Such a heart 'takes a deep interest in God's own life and is able, amid all its miseries, to resonate with the eternal innocence and eternal joy of God.'[b] In this spirituality, the invitation to begin by rejoicing in God's own mystery leads us to step back from ourselves and look from where the expectations and desires of a God who is love can receive a place of complementarity and reciprocity.

When an inner life is rebalanced in this way, with the heart opened and enlarged, it cannot be reduced just to 'father nostalgia'. Of course, attention to a reciprocity between human and divine desires may also include prayers of petition, but not without making them compatible with this mutual love. These prayers are no longer simply bargaining or emotional blackmail, but a shared concern between two who love one another, a common hope and a mutual viewpoint of love.[29] Everything is motivated and animated by that single mutual love, which henceforth is primary. Everything else must be consumed in the fire of that mutual love: the remains of a natural religiosity under all sorts of guises, be it 'father nostalgia', bargaining with God to the point of blackmail, a narrow moralism to the detriment of an inner life, many conditions to be fulfilled in order to approach God and be loved by him or concerns about efficacy and success even in spiritual matters. One single criterion will count in this mutual love, a single unique reality to which all others will progressively become subject: the quality of love given and received, in the inner life as in life itself.

If we are on our guard against such natural religiosity, each of us – whether we lead an inner life or not – will have the chance to free our representation of God from the conditioning imposed

---

a *Sagesse d'un pauvre*, Paris, Desclée de Brouwer, 1991, pp. 78–79, 106–107.

b Ibid, p. 106.

by 'father nostalgia', in which God is only there to respond to human demands and anguish. That vigilance enables us to envisage the possible existence in God himself of desires, among which the desire to be loved is not the least. Indeed, the presence of that divine desire cannot be suspected without a minimum of mutual attention, which could also lead each of us on towards reciprocal love for its own sake.

A God who Wants to be Loved

The second block to recognising that God himself wants to be loved comes from the almost exclusive insistence in a certain type of theological reflection, on the sacrificial and disinterested nature of divine love. This insistence not only tends to rarefy mediations about the desires a God of love might himself feel. Above all, it leads to the – perhaps unintentional – depiction of divine love that is closer to a kind of condescension than to proper love. For love is characterised by a personal intimacy, in which the desires of each have the right to be heard and together constitute the basis of a healthy reciprocity. There is a real risk of disfiguring divine love and also the divine–human love to which a God of love might aspire. That makes it important to challenge the appropriateness of any condescending representation of divine love.[30]

Throughout history many representations of God have been conditioned, sometimes without realising it, by an argument that the theologian Anders Nygren sums up thus: 'God feels no need. Therefore he has no desire, no aspiration. He cannot raise himself higher than he is already. So there can be no question of God's love for humanity, because that would mean God lowering himself from his divine perfection and bliss towards an inferior reality.'[a] This argument bears the marks of a whole philosophical heritage according to which God, who theoretically has no needs, does not feel any desire. This idea is already present in Plato in

---

a *Être et Agape*, Paris, Aubier, vol. 1, p. 237.

the fourth century BC. Plato was convinced that because of the perfection of the divine nature, God could not lack anything at all and applied the following principle very rigorously to his concept of the divine Being: 'He who desires desires something that he lacks and does not desire what he does not lack.'[a] The greatest philosophers of antiquity followed in his wake and only thought about desire and God in terms of the human being's desire for God and not of God's desire for human beings.[31] They ended up representing God as inward-looking, impassive, cold and abstract, a representation sometimes caricatured as 'the God of the philosophers'.

Is it necessary to recall that the influence of Greek philosophy was considerable, including on those first Christian thinkers – the 'church Fathers' – who tried to detach themselves from it in many ways? Christian theology ought to react against this 'God of the philosophers', because Christian faith looks to a God who is not introverted but turns towards his creatures to be united with them and offer them his love. However, the history of thought has often shown that even the fact of reacting against this or that approach sometimes comes down to thinking in terms of the categories of the approach concerned and remaining dependent on them. This means lacking sufficient inner freedom to approach the question from different angles, and open up to new, more enlightening horizons. That dialectic between the question of God and need, lack, desire has probably reinforced the tendency of a certain Christian theology to refrain from talking about a God who experiences a lack of love, and who created human beings in order to supply this lack for his own sake. This omission carries three risks: the risk of only stressing the sacrificial and disinterested aspect of divine love, a love that is only concerned with the happiness of the other, the attention paid to the other, looking out for the other. Then there is the risk of opposing certain aspects of the mystery of love that are not in opposition to each other, that is, on the one hand, the desire to give and to love, and on

---

a   *Le Banquet*, pp. 200–201. [Plato's *Banquet*, translated by Percy Bysshe Shelley, is available online.]

the other hand, the desire to receive and be loved. Lastly, there is the risk of confusing, consciously or unconsciously, the desire to be loved with a form of selfishness, to the point of excluding it, from the outset, from any representation of God. Because of this triple risk, it is important to bring out the two principal gaps in the philosophical reasoning set out earlier, gaps which have left their mark on theological thinking to this day. On the one hand, there is a conception of divine perfection that is too dependent on the problem of need and lack. On the other, the link between the notions of need, lack and desire becomes too reductionist and does not take sufficient account of the inherent complexity in the psychology of desire.

The way the thinkers concerned linked divine perfection with notions of need or lack shows how they were in the grip of the unconscious projection of which we spoke earlier, relating to a thirst for distant grandeur. All their reflection is centred on autonomy, whose highest expression consists in not needing anything or anybody and rejoicing in this self-sufficiency. From a psychological point of view, the true realisation of autonomy lies in the will and capacity to conduct relationships that are as harmonious as possible. This invites us to stop concentrating on the question of need and lack, in order to consider more fully the internal dynamism in any relationship tending towards love. When we take into account this impulse that love has, the impulse to love without ceasing, desire without ceasing, we perceive another dimension to the genesis of desire within an interpersonal relationship. Desire does not arise from a need as such, but fits more subtly into the dynamic and development of the particular relationship. If the relationship is going towards love, at some time or another it is bound to foster stronger and stronger reciprocal desires.[32] In other words, the development of reciprocal desires has more to do with the true nature of love growing within the interpersonal relationship than from the necessity inherent in a need pure and simple.

Moreover, within mature love, growth of the desire to love and the desire to be loved end up becoming inseparable, inextricable and continually feeding upon one another. Desire to be loved is

as much part of the splendour of reciprocal love as the desire
to love.[33] When we know and recognise one of the noblest and
finest aspirations of all, we should learn to stop discrediting and
neglecting it – in ourselves,[34] the other or God! We should also
learn how to free ourselves from the tendency to confuse this
desire to be loved with a form of selfishness. In fact, the desire
to be loved does not sink into selfishness unless it is no longer
or insufficiently accompanied by the desire to love the other
and contribute to his or her happiness. On the contrary, if the
desire to love is no longer accompanied by the desire to be loved,
it may become a kind of condescension, which also disfigures
the mystery of love. Love reaches its highest expression when
it harmoniously balances the desire to love and the desire to be
loved, and not when it leaves out the one or the other. Perhaps
that is the secret of its essence. Love loves and wants to be loved,
love can only love and want to be loved, love cannot stop loving
and wanting to be loved! If we try to relate this to transcendent
divine love, we must be careful to give both these aspects of the
mystery of love their rightful place. Then these will reach their
highest degree of intensity in the heart of God who, as supreme
Source of love, can only want to love his creature intensely and
be intensely loved in return.

As for the objection that the desire to be loved by human
beings would be an unworthy self-abasement on God's part
because, according to the terms used by Anders Nygren, it would
mean God 'lowering himself from his divine perfection and bliss
towards an inferior reality', it is so impregnated with the unconscious projection of a desire for dominant or distant grandeur
that it forgets two fundamental truths. First, love's only unworthy
self-abasement – even more so in divine love – would be not to
love enough and not to want to be loved enough. Second, unless
they are still very immature, someone seeking to love never thinks
of the beloved as an 'inferior reality', for notions of inferiority
and superiority are alien to love. In the eyes of a mature, realistic
love, there are neither inferior nor superior beings, but only loved
ones. Far from these theological currents, which often betray
an unconscious transference of human attributes commonly

assigned to hierarchical grandeur, St Bernard of Clairvaux was not wrong when he said, in the twelfth century, in his moving commentaries on the Song of Songs, where he compares God to a 'husband' and the soul to a 'wife: 'Love knows no respect for rank. The word "love" comes from "loving" not "honouring" [...] And this Husband, who has everything that might call for honour, admiration or even fear, greatly prefers being loved. Husband and wife are for each other. So what other reason or what other bond should be sought for between husband and wife but reciprocal love?'[a]

---

a Invitatés aux noces, from *Sermons sur le Cantique des cantiques*, translated and presented by Pierre-Yves Émery, Paris, Desclée de Brouwer, 1979, p. 158.

At the Heart of Unconditional Love

Among the theological blocks leading to this almost exclusive insistence on the sacrificial and disinterested aspect of divine love, there is one which requires particular attention, as its motivations are connected to one of Christ's most innovative messages. To understand the true nature of this block, we need first to look more closely at that message and the change of perspective it entails in the spiritual history of humanity. This message is the announcement of divine love offered to all without any conditions to be fulfilled, an unconditional, gratuitous love, that does not depend on any human merit but on God's mercy. 'When the goodness and loving-kindness of God our Saviour appeared, he saved us not because of any works of righteousness that we had done, but according to his mercy', Paul writes[a] and does not hesitate to sum up his confidence in a succinct formula: 'So it depends not on human will or exertion, but on God who shows mercy.'[b]

From the beginning, many forms of wisdom, spirituality and religious currents of all kinds have naturally been led to present a relationship with the supreme Being or a union with the Ultimate, or communion with God, not as a gift offered and accessible to all from the outset, but as a reward after a long journey reserved

---

a   Tit 3:4–5. See also Eph 2:4–5 and 9.
b   Rom 9: 16.

for the spiritual elite – a reward for merit, effort, ascesis, for perfection hedged about with endless requirements. Contrariwise, Christ's attitude towards people thought in his day to be the most distant from God because of the lives they led, their behaviour and beliefs, could be expressed in these words: 'You are already loved by God, whoever you are and whatever your past may be. So let him love you, dare to accept his love from now on, and gradually find healing for the secret wounds of your heart. Draw from this love the joy of making life sweet in your turn for those entrusted to you.' In Christ's eyes, love of neighbours is not a condition to be fulfilled in order to be loved by God, but a consequence of the astonishing and joyful discovery of being already loved by God.

This turnaround is how the apostle John writes about God: 'In this is love, not that we loved God but that he loved us [...] We love because he first loved us.'[a] This is a God whose very essence is love, that is to say, a God who can only love and let his love shine on all of us, who 'makes his sun rise on the evil and the good',[b] says Christ in his direct message, which St John, probably his closest disciple, sums up clearly: 'This is the message we have heard from him and proclaim to you, God is light and in him there is no darkness at all.'[c] But it is not surprising that such a radical reversal, so far removed from a certain human logic, should have encountered so much resistance, not only from within the religious movement of the time, but also today, even within Christian communities themselves. The tendency keeps coming back to reimpose such and such a condition to be fulfilled in order to receive divine love. It forgets that this love is offered first to those who were thought to be distant from it. 'Those who are well have no need of a physician, but those who are sick. Go and learn what this means, "I desire mercy, not sacrifice."'[d] This resistance becomes even stronger because it is rooted deep

---

a   1 Jn 4:10 and 19.

b   Mt 5:45.

c   1 Jn 1:5.

d   Mt 9:12–13.

in the vague guilt feeling and the real difficulty in believing we are worthy to be loved that we spoke about in Part 2 of this book. There was a long list of obstacles to overcome in order to learn how to become reconciled with ourselves, to discover ourselves to be wounded, and then arrive at a representation of God who knows this and only asks to heal our wounds, instead of increasing them by means of a superficial judgment.

We need to bear all this in mind to understand the hesitation of a Christian theology consistent with the gospel to stress the presence in God himself of a desire to be loved. That fear is understandable, given the omnipresence of the natural human tendency continually to reintroduce conditions to be fulfilled in order to be loved by God. An insistence on the presence in God himself of an expectation of being loved might even reactivate that process if it, too, was seen as a requirement whose satisfaction was necessary for the gift of divine love. Beset by this highly laudable concern, some great spiritual masters go so far as to say that God expects nothing in return, thereby fostering, perhaps unknowingly, the previously criticised representation of a God whose love is condescending. It is important not to oppose realities that are not in opposition to one another and, in particular, to grasp that their subtle articulation reveals more clearly both the beauty belonging to this unconditional aspect of God's love and the beauty belonging to his desire to be loved – a desire to be loved which we have already seen is as much part of the grandeur of love as the desire to love.

In fact, the divine offer of unconditional love does not imply that this love expects nothing in return, because the double basis of its gratuitousness is not affected by the presence in God himself of the expectation of being loved. Its first basis consists in the fact that this divine love precedes the human response and it remains true even if a positive response is ardently desired. Its second basis consists in the fact that this God of love will continue to love human beings and to knock at the door of our hearts, whatever the response he receives. That also remains true even though a positive response is ardently desired. Establishing this double basis allows us to see more clearly how God's desire to be loved relates to the gratuitousness of his unconditional love.

Although he so ardently desires a positive response from human beings, that is not because it is a condition to be fulfilled in order to be loved by God, but rather because it remains the only way of establishing a mutual communion of love. This communion requires the free choice of both, without which no relationship can really develop and flourish. In the eyes of God, who wants to love his creature intensely and be loved in return, nothing is more important that establishing a truly reciprocal love, respecting the freedom and otherness of each. At the heart of this unconditional love and this divine desire to be loved, there is indeed an invitation to enter into a reciprocal love experienced for its own sake, an urgent appeal to all and to each of us in particular.

Anyone who has gradually overcome the obstacles in the way of the difficult recognition of a desire to be loved in God himself, may be astonished to discover or rediscover how far the Bible itself movingly bears witness to this divine desire, in particular through Christ's appeal to the 'greatest and first commandment':[a] 'You shall love the Lord your God with all your heart, with all your soul and with all your mind.'[b] These are perhaps the words of the Bible that are both the best known and the most misunderstood. The three obstacles we have described, associated with unconscious projections of a dominant or distant grandeur, often do not allow us to hear the great cry of love hidden behind this call. These words have nearly always been understood and commented on as a revelation of the ultimate meaning of human life, of that towards which it should be directed, to the point of forgetting that the Bible is also and above all a revelation of the very mystery of God. 'The first and greatest commandment' itself contains a startling revelation about God. The very first demand addressed by God to his creatures, is not to do this or that particular work, to follow this or that narrow moral path or to adopt this or that pious stance. But it is to love him, God, and love him with our whole self! This reveals the heart of a God who ardently desires to be loved and loved not with a partial or

---

a   Mt 22:38.

b   Mt 22:37.

casual love but with a love that is total and passionate! Whatever our beliefs about religion, we have to admit that these biblical words contain an astonishing call, a call that is deeply moving. Every sincere request to be loved is moving. That emotion may reach great heights when the request comes from a person whose sensitivity and inner beauty are particularly highly developed. According to Christian revelation, this is an appeal from the supreme Source of love, from the most sensitive and loving Being there is, an intimately personal appeal addressed to each of us.

A God who desires to be intensely loved. Whether we are believers, non-believers or seekers, each of us is challenged by such a representation of God. It challenges the foundations of habitual ideas when the question of God is evoked. For those already leading an inner life, this divine desire remains an invitation to get rid of the remains of the distant condescension, so characteristic of the most widespread spontaneous representations of God. It enables them to advance further along the road of authentic divine–human reciprocity, where the double movement that constitutes love – loving and being loved – can henceforth tend entirely towards its highest degree of intensity. This call by God to be intensely loved invites them to ask themselves each day how they can now offer him their most intimate loving energies. The possible flowering of this reciprocity is greatly increased, because the happiness of the loved one depends closely upon the response given to his intimately personal expectations. The quality of this response is bound up with the degree of understanding and clarity about the expectations of the other. Thus the attention given to the sensitivity and expectations of this mysterious divine Presence[35] finally arouses a behaviour comparable to that of a man discovering with wonder the sensibility and expectations of the woman he loves. He becomes even more aware, motivated and stimulated to offer her a high quality of love. That awareness, motivation and stimulation are essential to promote the progressive integration of human feeling and emotion and way of loving into a relationship with God – an integration that leads that reciprocal love gradually to reach a degree of intensity it has never known before.[36]

An Unexpected Capacity to Love

The fourth block to recognising God's own desire to be loved is the difficulty, experienced more or less strongly by each of us, in recognising our own inner beauty, especially the hidden beauty of our capacity to love. Indeed, the more we doubt our power to love, the more difficult it becomes to suspect that a God of love would appreciate it in us, to the point of wanting to be loved by us. Even after we have seriously taken into account the influence of secret wounds, that so often prevent each of us from seeing our own inner beauty and that of others,[a] the question remains: How can a human being be up to loving the supreme Source of love itself, whose essence corresponds to the ultimate, transcendent expression of love? How can we be capable of loving the most sensitive and loving Being of all, seeing that we already find it so difficult to make those people happy to whom we are closest here below?

Reciprocal divine–human love may seem so improbable that many spiritualities have refused to envisage or recognise even the possibility of its happening in this world. That refusal is another reason to ask on what grounds Christian theology dares to believe in this possibility for human beings to enter as of now into reciprocal love with God, a reciprocal love which, of course, will only reach its fulfilment in eternity. No one will be surprised

---

a   See 'A God who Knows Each One's Wounds' in Part 2 of this book.

that it is not based upon the vagaries of human subjectivity. That subjectivity is wracked with doubts, following sometimes painful experiences. It is ever ready to stop at appearances and to play tricks on anyone who takes it for the only guide. However, many will be surprised to discover that behind its simple, even naïve, formulation, belief in reciprocal divine–human love has a depths and coherence beyond what might have been suspected at first. In fact, it is one of the most ancient biblical beliefs, a belief with considerable repercussions for confidence in a mysterious divine–human correspondence, thanks to which a reciprocal relationship between the Creator and his creature can be conceived. 'God created humankind in his own image, in the image of God he created them; male and female he created them.'[a] That belief is the foundation not only for the compatibility between this Creator-God and his creature, but also the human potential for loving that enables us one day to rise to the level of divine love. Traces of this potential for loving are recognisable from the presence in each of us of an unquenchable yearning to be loved and to love, which seeks to blossom if it finds itself in circumstances favourable to its full expression. But only the creation of this potential for loving in God's image can support confidence in the possibility of reciprocal divine–human love. Finally, trying to deepen this belief means going right to the heart of our confidence in an exceptional power to love dormant in each human being. Even when it is provisionally damaged or paralysed by the hardness of life, it is still present and constitutes our most genuine identity. Trying to deepen this belief means being invited to look at the human capacity to love in a way that renews our own view of our own power to love.

The considerable range of this belief cannot, however, be deepened today without first confronting its most obvious detractors. It has been so often criticised, even derided by certain trends of atheist thought. This criticism was, in fact, a decisive turning point in the history of modern atheism, in the nineteenth century with Ludwig Feuerbach, who could, in many respects,

---

a   Gen 1:27.

be considered as the true father of the theory of unconscious projection and its application to faith in God. In fact, he remains the principal instigator of the suspicion, most often voiced by atheism towards any kind of theological reflection, that in their spiritual quest human beings merely create a 'god' in their own image. That suspicion is just the clever inversion of the belief that God created human beings in his image. Having established the omnipresence of this self-projection process in many representations of God, Ludwig Feuerbach ends up being persuaded that God does not exist, that 'God is the mirror of man'[a] that 'the divine being is nothing but the essence of humanity'[b], before concluding that 'religion, at least the Christian religion, is the relationship of man with himself, or more precisely with his essence, but with his essence as with that of another being'.[c] He carried many illustrious thinkers in his wake – according to the confession of Friedrich Engels, for a time we were all 'Feuerbachians'[d] – beginning with Karl Marx and Sigmund Freud, who followed the thought of the great philosopher on this point, even though they followed their own particular bent and carried it into their own preferred sphere.

However, by relying on the projection theory to justify their atheism, Ludwig Feuerbach and his disciples overstepped a mark, which reason on its own does not allow. There is a major distinction between the question of the representation of God and the question of God's existence. Even if the influence of all the possible and imaginable unconscious projections proved to go further than everything that has been discovered so far, this would only challenge the *representation* of God and not the existence of God as such. Drawing hasty conclusions about God's non-existence from projection theory is to overstep the bounds of reason, as the theologian Walter Kasper notes: 'From the fact

a *L'essence du christianisme*, Paris, Gallimard, 1992, p. 188.

b Ibid, p. 131.

c Ibid, p. 131.

d *Ludwig Feuerbach et la fin de la philosophie classique allemande*, Paris, Éditions Sociales, 1945, p. 12.

of projection we can simply deduce an undeniably subjective element in our knowledge, but nothing about the actual reality of the object experienced and known. With the help of projection theory, we can certainly explain subjective representations of God to a certain extent, but we can say nothing about the reality of God himself.'[a] In this respect, the ease with which projection theory was sometimes appropriated in order to deny God's existence is comparable to the ease with which the theory of evolution was sometimes appropriated with the same aim.[37] This seems to be a way of wrongly using human sciences or exact sciences as an excuse to get rid of the very idea of God, as a kind of score settling. Doubtless, the idea of God is judged to be too revolting, distressing or disturbing for the person concerned.[38]

The suspicion that in their spiritual quest human beings merely create a God in their own image must be challenged by anyone trying to establish the most reliable contribution of projection theory. It goes without saying that human beings cannot apprehend a given reality, of whatever nature or belonging to whatever sphere, except through categories and elements which they know from a practical or theoretical point of view. Any apprehension of reality necessarily consists of projections and transferences, so that it is never the objective reality as such that is perceived, but a more or less successful approach to its true identity. This applies even more so to representation of God because each of us only has human notions and images with which to conceive a reality that, by definition, does not belong to this earthly state. Consequently, the discernment to be exercised in this sphere does not lie in determining whether or not projections intervene within representations of God. Of course, they do! But then we have to determine how far they constitute a legitimate approach to the mystery concerned or, on the contrary, a disfiguration that is harmful to our quest. Moreover, this discernment must first distinguish between unconscious projections and consciously chosen projections in order to come to terms with such a mystery. Before deciding whether these conscious projections are

---

a   *Le Dieu des chrétiens*, Paris, Cerf, 1985, p. 53.

compatible with the belief in question, we have to identify and set aside the unconscious projections which may lead our quest astray from the outset. That is why this book has tried to make a systematic double check, first, by unmasking certain tricks played by these unconscious processes and, second, by checking the coherence of deliberately chosen representations of God with a belief in a God of love. The analysis of unconscious projections of the infantile desire for omnipotence, the harsh self-view, the thirst for domineering or distant grandeur have certainly given spectacular examples of the risk run by human beings of creating a God in their own image. But, above all, it has brought out the extent of the inner conversion needed to pass from these spontaneous religious representations to a coherent representation of the God of love proclaimed by Christian revelation.[39] That coherent representation of a God of love is made possible by insights that are sometimes hard won and sometimes astonishing. It forbids the simplistic identification of any representation of God with an illusion, produced by unconscious projections by means of which human beings merely create a God in their own image.[40]

However, many thinkers who regard the belief that 'God created humankind in his own image' as a naïve idea, just asking to be turned the other way round, have not primarily been lacking in that discernment. What they have lacked most has been careful reflection on the link between the ultimate aim pursued by this God of love and the creation of humankind in his image, which gives the belief that God created humans in his own image a rarely suspected depths and coherence. Indeed, if, as Christian revelation holds, there really exists a God whose aim is to create a conscious being who can one day enjoy eternal reciprocal love with him, then the creation of humankind in his own image is simply indispensable to the fulfilment of his plan. This God of love would have found it impossible to have such a relationship with humanity, if he had not taken care that the human race should be capable of expecting and offering a love corresponding to his own![41] In view of the impressive precision that characterises so many elements, properties and constants in the Universe, or the subtle coordination and prodigious creative ingenuity that have operated throughout evolution, it seems highly improbable that the dimension that was the most essential, that which justified the existence of all the others, should have been the most neglected. For Christian spirituality, confidence in the hidden beauty of every human being, confidence in their potential for love, is rooted in confidence in the coherence of this divine project. The creation of humankind was designed to make them capable of reciprocal love with God. Only that mysterious correspondence between divine and human ways of expecting and offering love could make possible such a divine–human reciprocity. How could this God of love have called upon humanity to love him with all their heart, had he not taken care that they should have had an unexpected capacity to love?

'I am Wonderfully Made, Wonderful are your Works'

'I am wonderfully made, wonderful are your works', the psalmist dares to exclaim![a] Let there be no mistake. There is no trace in this awestruck confidence of any kind of pride. Rather, the psalmist expresses genuine humility that leads him to place his confidence not in his own subjective impressions, but in the project that this Creator-God, of whom the Bible says that he 'saw everything that he had made, and indeed, it was very good.'[b] Let there be no mistake. There is no trace in this awestruck confidence of a blindness that would deny the presence in humankind of various limitations, weaknesses, struggles and wounds. Rather, there is a clarity that has learnt to recognise the presence in each of us of a potential for love that is even deeper than these various limitations, weaknesses, struggles and wounds[42] – a potential for love that really only seeks the chance to blossom. Let there be no mistake. There is no trace in this awestruck confidence of ignorance or relativisation of the evil committed by ourselves or by others. Rather, there is a capacity to discern, even behind this evil, a yearning to be loved and to love, a yearning whose sufferer has been wounded. It recalls that even the most reprehensible actions do not prove that their doer was evil in himself, but that he may have felt he was not understood, recognised and loved as

---

a   Ps 139:14.

b   Gen 1:31.

much as he would have liked. It recalls that any behaviour judged to be reprehensible – the cause of our doubts about our own inner beauty or that of others – paradoxically takes us back to a wound that has not healed, which, in turn, takes us back to damaged feelings, which, in turn again, take us back to disappointed expectations, which, in turn yet again, take us back to the greatness of this yearning to be loved and to love that is so characteristic of the inner beauty of each of us![43] It recalls that looking clearly at human difficulties, slowness, stumbling and mistakes along this long road of continual apprenticeship in love does not stop our believing in the human potential to love. As with any potential that has not had the chance to operate in favourable conditions, it does not mean that because this potential for love has not shown in its best light, we must conclude that it does not exist.

This clear view is the view of Christ himself in his capacity to discern, even under the appearances of evil, the secret wounds of others, wounds that he helped to heal by the gift of his love. At the same time he invited people he met in this way to continue learning how to love. The compassion and love so characteristic of his attitude remain the sign that these calls to love – even at their most demanding – should not be interpreted as a lack of understanding of human wounds, a lack of respect for the time each of us needs to heal bit by bit, as conditions to be fulfilled in order to benefit from his love, or as a burden he lays on anyone's shoulders.[44] On the contrary, his appeals to love should be interpreted as a mark of confidence and encouragement, as an indirect revelation of that potential for love that he was able to find under the contradictions of the human heart, as a way of reassuring each of us about our inner beauty. 'Even at the moments when you doubt your capacity to love, know that I, Christ, continue to believe in you. I know your inner beauty, which is often not seen by others, which perhaps you do not even suspect yourself. It exceeds anything you can imagine because you are a marvel of consciousness and love, created in God's image in order to live in reciprocal love with him, and so you have everything necessary in order to do so. Dare to believe, not only in the divine love that is given to you as of now, but also in the treasures of love and tenderness that lie in the depths of your heart. They make you capable of responding to God's ardent desire to be loved by you. They will enable you to contribute to the happiness of the supreme Source of love itself.'[45] In the eyes of Christian theology, thanks to his shining love, Christ's life not only revealed the true face of God, which has so often been disfigured, but the true face of humanity, also so often disfigured. It considers that the full expression of this potential for love was manifested through Jesus' own humanity, and finds in it a confirmation of true human identity as a being really created in God's image, a being really capable of living in intense communion with God.

'I am wonderfully made, wonderful are your works': a magnificent vision of human beings, in which their most authentic identity and inner beauty are seen in the light of a theology that takes seriously the ultimate aim pursued by this God of love and its concrete repercussions on human beings made in his image. This vision shows the extent of the change of heart a mature Christian faith needs to undergo in relation to a certain historical Christianity which tried to magnify God's grandeur by systematically denigrating human beings,[46] without realising that this actually disfigured the face of its own faith. A certain kind of catechesis overdid the laying on of guilt, which in many respects was a manipulation of consciences,[47] and led many believers to find it difficult to believe themselves worthy of being loved, happy and joyful. That inner difficulty has always fostered those spiritualities based on privation, renunciation, humiliation and other so-called 'pious' practices, whose ambiguity provoked Friedrich Nietzsche's scathing remark: 'The only way they could love God was by crucifying man.'[a] Such a running down of humanity reinforced the representation of a sadistic God, who was jealous not only of human pleasure and happiness, but also of human knowledge and reason. The tendency to run down humanity caused a growing opposition, from the Renaissance onwards, between theological thinking and humanism, as well as the sciences. This opposition ended up driving many illustrious

---

a   *Ainsi parla Zarathustra*, Paris, Aubier, 1946, p. 197.

thinkers into seeing only one possible way out of the continual
tensions: to proclaim 'the death of God', so that human beings
could live and flourish fully, according to Friedrich Nietzsche's
incantations: 'This God is dead! Superior men, this God is your
worst enemy [...] God is dead. But we now only want the living
Superman.'[a] Keeping this historical framework in mind makes us
value all the more a theology that takes the ultimate foundation
of human grandeur and beauty into account: being created in the
image of God in order to live with him in reciprocal love that will
have no end.[48] It also leads us to value all the more a theology
that is really in accord with belief in a God of love, a theology
sufficiently aware that such a God, like anyone who truly loves,
could only rejoice greatly in everything that leads to the joy,
pleasure and happiness of the loved one.

Rebelling against a representation of God that seemed to be
synonymous with suffering, death, renunciation of joy and life,
the negation of the beauty of existence and human greatness,
Friedrich Nietzsche proclaimed through his Zarathustra: 'I can
only believe in a God who can dance.'[b] Doubtless he would have
appreciated the strong stress on joy and dancing in this biblical
text from the prophet Zephaniah: '[Your God] will rejoice over
you with happy song, he will renew you by his love, he will
dance with shouts of joy for you';[c] or the fresco in the Church
of St Saviour in Chora, in Istanbul, in which Christ dances as he
saves humanity. The theologian Olivier Clément comments thus:
'Christ descends into hell, with one foot he kicks down the gates
of hell; with the other he steps upwards in dazzling whiteness,
snatching Adam and Eve from their tombs! There we have it,
"the dancing God"! And the Christian is someone who dances
for joy because he knows love is stronger than death.'[d] And for a
really mature Christian faith that is the most beautiful dance to
which the human heart is invited: to dance for joy at having been

---

a   Ibid, pp. 551–553.

b   Ibid, p. 107.

c   Zeph 3:17.

d   *Taizé, un sens de la vie*, op.cit., p. 31.

created to live in eternal reciprocal love and to possess all the inner beauty, all the necessary potential for love to dare to begin as of today. And to dance for our even greater happiness and that of a God of love, who is surely the first to wish that our inner life and life here below, with all the love that each can contain, tends each day towards their highest degree of intensity.[49]

'I am wonderfully made, wonderful are your works'. This confident amazement frees people from the partly unconscious conditioning that often drives them – whether they call themselves 'believers' or not – to picture divine transcendence as distant condescension. It is the goal of a journey that gradually unfolds a completely different representation of divine transcendence from that suggested by unconscious projections of a thirst for domineering or distant grandeur – a journey punctuated by numerous calls to transform representations that are most incompatible with the mystery of a God whose essence is love. It shows three essential foundations to a possible divine–human reciprocal love, four pillars on which Christian mysticism invites us to build the castle of our inner life: the living awareness that the true greatness of a God of love lies in the quality of his love, that is always on offer, and not in a domineering, even crushing, attitude; the living awareness that it is no longer a question of divine transcendence wanting to keep its distance in cold self-sufficiency, but on the contrary, a divine transcendence wanting to come close to each of us at every moment – whether or not we feel its presence[50] – in order to invite us to enter into reciprocal love for its own sake; the living awareness that a God of love can only want to be intensely loved himself and this overwhelming appeal, addressed to each of us, remains an invitation to love God with our whole self, and continually to integrate our own humanity, feelings, emotions, yearning to be loved into our inner lives; lastly, the living awareness that a Creator-God, determined to create a being capable of a life of love with him, has necessarily seen to it that each of us has the potential for loving, a way of expecting and offering love that corresponds sufficiently to his own, so that his plan may be capable of fulfilment. This myste-rious divine–human correspondence is the ultimate foundation of the confidence that it is possible for each of us, without exception, to enter as of now into a reciprocal life of love, with our heart just as it is, with its expectations and desires just as they are, with that deep, strong yearning to be loved and to love, which only seeks to blossom and take this divine–human union to its highest level.

PART 4

Misunderstood Aspects of an even Greater Love

Unconscious Projections and Representations of Divine Tenderness

Certain unconscious projections graft themselves onto the mental images aroused by theological language when that language – inevitably – resorts to human analogies to evoke a mystery whose nature is of another order. There is no doubt about it: representations of God using this or that analogy – the father figure, for example – unleash in each of us unconscious projections, linked to our personal history, psychological profile and sexual identity. Under the influence of these projections, some people will keep their distance from a God who recalls all too strongly the unhealed wounds of their childhood and youth. Others will systematically reject any spiritual perspective, which they have made the scapegoat for a personal score settling. Still others will only lead their inner lives through the prism of the only analogy they have retained from their religious education or the surrounding culture, with this double risk: either the analogy in question is linked, consciously or unconsciously, to a negative experience in their lives and therefore risks preventing their relationship with God going beyond a certain level of confidence and intimacy; or the analogy in question is linked, consciously or unconsciously, to a positive experience in their lives and then the risk is that it will foster a conception of God that is reduced to that single aspect, to the detriment of other aspects of this divine mystery.

A God of love can only want to lead his creatures into ever deeper confidence and intimacy with himself, inviting them to discover constantly that his divine love is greater still, his divine tenderness goes beyond anything human beings have been led to believe. When we realise these risks, we may learn discernment with regard to human analogies used in so much that is said about God, to take into account the cultural, psychological and theological conditioning that is inevitably involved, to be clear about their advantages and disadvantages, to free ourselves from spontaneous representations of God whose exclusive link to this or that analogy makes it difficult to access other aspects of the mystery of a God who is love. As this fourth part of the book gradually unmasks these unconscious projections, it will make other misunderstood aspects of this divine love accessible, and reveal their power to promote the full flowering of a reciprocal divine–human love.

High Stakes

In order to evoke the mystery of a God whose identity corresponds with the ultimate source of love, the use of analogies relative to a human way of being and loving must try to avoid two very common extremes. The first consists in projecting human attributes too completely onto the divine attributes, as if it were a matter of course that these were identical in all respects. This extreme does not sufficiently take into account the fact that the mystery of a Creator-God, by his very divine nature, cannot belong to the same dimensions as his own creation. The creatures' constitutive elements are not in the same sphere. The other extreme consists in stressing the previous point so strongly that we deny the mystery of the Creator-God can have any correspondence at all with the mystery of human beings. This extreme does not sufficiently take into account the fact that a Creator-God owed it to himself to create a conscious being whose way of expecting and offering love sufficiently corresponded to his own, if he wanted reciprocal divine–human love to become a reality. In the light of this divine project, we see the link between Paul's assertion that 'God chose us in Christ before the foundation of the world to be holy and blameless before him in love'[a] and the biblical vision of creation: 'God created humankind in his own image, in the image of God he created them; male and female he created them.'[b][51]

---

a Eph 1:4.

b Gen 1:27.

Of course, the degree of this mysterious divine–human correspondence cannot be measured, but its existence is still the
ultimate basis and justification for the use in theological thinking
of analogies with the human way of being and loving. When they
are used in a way that is compatible with the reciprocal love
sought by this Creator-God, and do not disfigure the quality of
love proper to such a God, such analogies should not be reduced
to simple linguistic tricks, whose only reason for use is the
human incapacity to do without them here below. They must be
considered as a legitimate approach to a divine mystery that goes
beyond them without thereby being alien to them

The notion of mystery also adds a criterion for the fruitful use
of human analogies in theological propositions. Contrary to the
meaning sometimes given to it in common speech, a mystery is
not something that cannot be understood but something that
can never be *completely* understood. Applied to the mystery of a
God who is love, this distinction is all the more essential because
such a God can only rejoice in constantly revealing new aspects
of his divine love to human beings. Consequently, although it
is important to recognise behind an appropriate analogy a real
ability to approach the mystery of a God of love, it is equally
important to overcome the risk of only seeing this divine love
from the perspective of that single analogy, to the detriment of
other approaches that can reflect different aspects of its mystery.

These criteria for discernment show that the stakes are high.
Their concrete repercussions on any quest for meaning or any
spiritual experience have not always been seen clearly. When we
discover or rediscover these one by one, we are challenged by
them and then give ourselves a way of meeting that challenge.
For those who regard themselves as non-believers, the challenge
is not to remain indifferent or even hostile to the question of
God because of an analogy sometimes instilled in childhood,
which sets up a block for personal reasons, when this representation, often more of a caricature, only corresponds, at best, to a
reductionist aspect of the divine mystery. For those who regard
themselves as believers, the challenge is not to remain conditioned
by this or that theological representation to such an extent that

they can no longer open themselves up to other possible aspects of the mystery of a God of love, to other possible ways of being loved by God and loving God.[52]

Overcoming Reductionist Cultural Conditioning

Among the possible analogies available to us here below to reflect different aspects of divine love, the most appropriate are naturally to be found in the most intense and beautiful loving relationships given to human beings: married love, parental love and fraternal love, which extends beyond the circle of actual brothers and sister to friends. However, in every era and in every society, theological reflection has always borne the mark of a cultural and sociological heritage, which sometimes strongly conditions the representation of God. In this respect, globalisation, the intermingling of cultures, interdisciplinary exchanges between researchers from all over the world in the exact sciences as well as in the human sciences, with the resulting intellectual and spiritual opening up, offer twenty-first-century women and men the chance to look more objectively at cultural and theological conditioning upon which their predecessors were so dependent.

In the history of theology, by far the most spectacular cultural conditioning – and the most serious because of its many repercussions on the spiritual level – remains that of the patriarchal culture with its propensity to think of fatherhood and manhood as superior to motherhood and womanhood. That culture has largely contributed not only to keeping women subordinated in society, with many resulting inequalities, but also to making it almost impossible to employ feminine imagery to represent a God, whose superiority to humanity was sometimes compared to the superiority men were thought to have over women![53] Under its influence the exclusive use of masculine analogies has so forged and shaped theological language over the centuries that many believers do not realise, even today, how reductionist and unjustifiable such usage is. That blindness may be typical of how a whole culture and way of thinking can condition people's minds, but it remains surprising, since the slightest effort of intellectual logic easily unmasks its deficiencies. From two considerations one fact emerges: either the mystery of a God of love is thought of as having no relation to the psychic reality of our sexual identity (not to be confused with organic sexuality), in which case there is no reason to use masculine analogies any more than feminine ones; or the mystery of a God of love is thought of as having a relation to the psychic reality of our sexual identity, in which case there is still no reason that this link should only exist with the masculine half of that reality! In both cases, the exclusive use of masculine analogies to evoke the mystery of God is unacceptable.

Clarity and vigilance with respect to this abusive and reductionist usage are all the more important as it has considerable repercussions upon an inner spiritual journey, because of the psychological attitude that this or that analogy arouses both in people who call themselves 'believers' and in those who call themselves 'non-believers'. In order to be convinced of this, we need only set two analogies side by side. Despite being something of a caricature and their somewhat provocative appearance, these two analogies have the merit of showing the power of a mental image and its repercussions in terms of interest, confidence, tenderness, response and personal implications. These inner dispositions will turn out very different according to whether someone thinks they are in the presence of an old man with a beard, with a severe expression and authoritarian gestures, or else in the presence of a delightful, welcoming and smiling young woman![54]

Integrating our Humanity into Reciprocal Love

The importance of exercising discernment in the use of masculine and feminine analogies within theological language has never been taken seriously enough in the course of history. This is not only because of the influence of patriarchal culture, but also because of a lack of knowledge about human functioning and in particular, human psychology, which saw tremendous advances during the nineteenth century.[55] Until then there prevailed a simplistic opposition between body and spirit, the conviction that they were two totally distinct realities, without any particular relation or unity. This was probably under the influence of Platonist thought, which had ended up even taking over Christian thinking, whose real roots lay in Hebrew thought that propounded a certain physical–psychic unity. The opposition between body and sprit led to a long neglect of the theme of sexual identity, because it was seen as merely a bodily reality and, therefore, superficial. However, among the great discoveries in psychology during the twentieth century was the importance of the part played by the psychic dimension of sexual identity in the formation of each personality, in its conduct of any interpersonal relationship and in particular its way of being and loving. Angelo Hesnard, a doctor who introduced psychoanalysis into France, wrote during the 1950s: 'Leaving aside for the moment the observation of the erotic function, when the psychologist seeks to know what, in both sexes, characterises sexual gender on the psychological level, he confirms the law expounded by physiologists with regard to organic sexuality: every apparent element of the personality is "sexualised" in the sense that it is influenced by the fact of the person being either a man or a woman. There is a masculine way and a feminine way of feeling and judging life, of feeling emotion (lower emotions like identifying with another – a child, a sick person or someone suffering – and higher ones such as religious exaltation or an aesthetic frisson), of acting in this or that circumstance, even of thinking philosophically.'[a]

The way in which each human being assumes their masculine or feminine identity (not forgetting that the man has a feminine side – the *anima* – and woman has a masculine side – the *animus*)[56] lies at the heart of every interpersonal relationship, including, therefore, the relationship in the spiritual sphere with God.[57] Rather than being reduced to a purely biological question linked to the reproduction of the species, sexual identity involves the whole person and determines even the deepest recesses of each person's feelings, particularly their expectation of being loved and of loving. It is an integral part of the mystery of each person,[58] this mystery of consciousness and love which, according to Christian revelation, God loves and wants to be intensely loved by. All who want to love God with their whole being, respond with every fibre of their being to the appeal of this God of love, have no other way to do so than to learn to integrate their humanity, their sensitivity, their expectation of being loved and loving – all inseparable from their sexual identity – into a reciprocal divine–human love which can then be experienced as fully as possible.[59] Ultimately, this shows one of the most essential issues in the use of masculine and feminine analogies within theological reflection: to awaken and sustain the maximum integration of our whole humanity into a reciprocal love of God, so that this love can reach its highest degree of intensity.[60]

---

a   *La sexologie*, Paris, Payot, pp. 221–222.

Actively Fostering Confidence
in being Loved

The desire to love such a God with one's whole self will only arise in a human heart when this has first been profoundly touched by that divine love. That raises the question of the transmission of this love. Every belief that recognises a link between the mystery of God and the mystery of love must constantly ask about the degree of confidence in God's love that its theological language may or may not be capable of increasing. Christian theology, which has set the revelation of this divine love at the heart of its faith, cannot underestimate the immensity of the challenge to be met, especially if it bears in mind the difficulty we humans have in believing we are worthy to be loved, the mountains of guilt and the various secret fears of God, which always find an opportunity to break out.

Here too we need discernment in order to use masculine and feminine analogies better, so that we do not disfigure a God whose very essence is love. It seems undeniable that the suppression of feminine analogies in theological reflection remains a handicap that is damaging to us all, because it deprives the representation of God of mental images that are also capable of paying homage to the beauty of his divine love, of actively fostering confidence in that love. We are not talking about fostering a naïve or excessive idealisation of the feminine way of being and loving. Such an idealisation would be just as symptomatic as its abusive suppression. Neither are we denying the disadvantages in the use of feminine analogies.

Of course, they are just as numerous as the disadvantages of using masculine analogies. But it is a question of recognising the appropriateness of feminine analogies to take into account certain dimensions of the mystery of love in a way that is both different and particularly beautiful. We start with tenderness, compassion, kindness, listening, comforting, or the unconditional gift of love characteristic of mother love.

The confidence and emotional attachment that the figure of Mary has inspired throughout the centuries, especially in Catholic and orthodox Christian communities but sometimes even beyond Christianity, are a striking example. However, Mary is not God and in many believers a passion for her cult often risks hiding two indirect disfigurements of a God who is love. For some, there is a secret fear of God – unadmitted or partly unconscious – since this smiling, welcoming feminine figure overflowing with tenderness that Mary is in their eyes apparently gives them more confidence than the representation they still make of God (doubtless derived from the strict, even harsh father, which is how God is mostly thought of). For others, an apparent difficulty in suspecting that that the highest expression of this Marian way of being and loving is to be found in God himself. These people are victims of spiritual reflection that for centuries has systematically and exclusively focused any feminine element on the figure of Mary. In fact, rather than contributing to the integration of feminine analogies into language about God, that focus has reinforced or sustained a false polarity between a feminine figure on the one hand, Mary, and a masculine figure on the other, God. However deeply rooted in the consciousness or the unconscious, this secret fear and false duality make it difficult to take in a reality which ought rather to be seen as an immediate consequence of the existence of a God whose essence corresponds to the ultimate expression of love. No one is better placed than this God to offer each of us a love that is overflowing with kindly understanding and tenderness, which is often what women are best at here below.[61]

That realisation means we must be careful that an integration of feminine analogies reflects the beauty of a God of love through all the aspects of woman and her mystery and not just through the images of the mother and the virgin, to which Mary has often been reduced. The challenge is even greater because of the double risk contained in the ambivalence of the mother figure in the human psyche and, more precisely, in the masculine psyche, as clinical psychology has constantly observed. On the one hand, the positive imprint of the mother image fosters the very real risk of a fusional attachment to the mother – unconsciously wanting her to be a virgin. This prevents a man from giving any real place to another woman in his inner life and his way of thinking. On the other hand, the negative imprint of the mother image, linked to the infant perception of the mother's terrifying omnipotence, recalls a humiliating and hated dependency, which may lead to a systematic repression of any imagery with a feminine connotation. This ambivalence reveals certain hidden complicities of a psychological nature, without which patriarchal culture on its own probably would not have been able to impose its law for so long in theological language, which, throughout the centuries, has been in the hands of men potentially exposed to this double risk.

We must bear in mind these many aspects of the challenge to make God's beauty also shine through analogies relative to a feminine way of being and loving. This gradually gives us discernment criteria so that we can finally give such analogies their complementary and reciprocal place. The exercise of this discernment will not leave indifferent those who have known the grace of glimpsing here below, through a love or a friendship that has really mattered in their personal life, the capacity of woman and her mystery to reflect the beauty of a God who is love. Neither will it leave indifferent those who remain both clear and careful about the absolute priority and the ultimate scope of language used by theology to try and convey God's love: actively to foster in one another the confidence that we are loved.

A Mystery to Discover and Explore Forever

We must add a third important challenge to the two previously mentioned, which promote confidence in being loved by God and promote the integration of our own expectation of being loved and loving into a reciprocal love of God. The third challenge is this: constant research and discovery of what might be characteristic of the mystery of a God of love. If by its very nature, the mystery of God can never be fully discovered and understood by human beings, should we still keep on the lookout for discoveries in the human sciences – among others – which could indirectly give us precious information in this quest? Taking into consideration the mysterious divine–human correspondence in love not only provides an ultimate justification for the use of human analogies we have already spoken about, but it also invites us to recognise that certain psychological discoveries relating to the human conduct of reciprocal love can be regarded as a source of indirect information about the mystery of a God who wants to live in reciprocal love with his creatures. Anyone who has experienced genuine love, even once in their lifetime, will agree. If our own expectation of being loved does not receive from the other a sufficiently compatible offer of love or if our own desire to love is not matched in the other by a sufficiently compatible desire to love, then there can be no long-term reciprocal love. So this is not an insignificant detail, but the very basis without which no love can really blossom. When it has been established that the psychological conduct of this expectation of being loved and loving is not separable in human beings from their sexual identity, a certain kind of compatibility between that sexual identity and the mystery of a God of love deserves to be taken more seriously into consideration. Of course, this compatibility should not be measured or reduced to human categories as such, but as one of the great twentieth-century theologians, the Dominican Yves Congar recalls: 'If "God created humankind in his own image, in the image of God he created them, male and female he created them" (Gen 1:27), there must be in God, in transcendent form, something that corresponds to masculinity and something that corresponds to femininity.'[a] This has to do not just with a single – although primordial – concern to sustain human beings in a reciprocal love relationship with God. The use of masculine and feminine analogies ultimately relates to the divine mystery that any spiritual quest and any theological research must constantly seek to discover more fully, that is, explore within an inner life, in an incessant dialogue with all the forms of knowledge about the deep identity of human beings.

Whatever people think about one or other of the multiple challenges we have previously mentioned, just one of these justifies an inquiry into the use of masculine and feminine analogies that are most fitted not to disfigure the tenderness of a God of love and, in particular, an inquiry into the integration of feminine analogies, whose shining and beauty are most capable of illuminating any attempt to express a reflection of this divine love. But just as a political reflection should not be content to deliver a correct diagnosis about possible problems in society without suggesting concrete and workable solutions, this theological reflection is also trying to suggest definite paths – though not exhaustive or exclusive ones – which can favour a clear and balanced use of masculine and feminine analogies. This rebalancing will aim to show not only that a sensible integration of feminine analogies is possible, but also that it is really capable

---

a   *Je crois en l'Esprit Saint*, Paris, Cerf, p. 721.

of renewing a lot of thinking – by believers or non-believers – about a God who is love.

Such a step can apply to numerous religious traditions.[62] Here we will start from the Christian mystery of the Trinity. Many find the Trinity too disconcerting, but thanks to its insistence on the existence in God himself of movements of love, of divine persons who love each other so much that this results in total unity with total respect for the otherness of persons, this mystery of the Trinity brings each of us, whether Christian or not, back to our own experience of love and invites us to ask the following question: how could there be a link between love and a divine mystery if that mystery only corresponded to an isolated solitude in heaven? Many find the Trinity too abstract, but thanks to the movements of interpersonal love that constitute it, this mystery gives divine–human love and human love a mystical scope synonymous with an ultimate meaning that could strongly motivate the long-term renewal of love. As it continues to unmask the most damaging unconscious projections in the search for meaning or an already developed inner life, this reflection will invite each of us to look again at such divine love and find in it a meaning to life or draw from it the motivation for the daily renewal and blossoming of human love as well as divine–human love.

Beyond the Father Figure

Incontestably, the father figure remains one of the images most often attributed to God by theological reflection through the ages, particularly in areas of the world impregnated with Judeo-Christian culture. It remains the figure most anchored in collective memory, that is, the first to come to mind when the question of God is raised. Among the psychological transferences attaching to this father figure, the most common rests on the confusion between ideas of divine fatherhood and human fatherhood, unconsciously taking each of us back to our own experience of a father. The most damaging consequences of such a transference affect mainly people who carry a negative father image, especially if they have had serious difficulties in their relationship with their own biological father. So there is a high probability that they will project certain features relating to the behaviour they suffered from during their childhood and adolescence onto their spontaneous representation of a Father-God. There are two possible repercussions, each as damaging as the other in the search for meaning. Either this projection paralyses any spiritual approach by fostering a more or less virulent rejection of a God who has become the scapegoat for the settling of personal scores. Or this projection disfigures their inner life by making it the prisoner of a God who is as illusory as he is tyrannical. Then those close to these prisoners will suffer from their God as well. Moreover, even without going into particular relationship difficulties, in many lives the father figure tends, symbolically or concretely, towards various forms of strictness, intransigence, distance or absence, all notions that risk blocking or slowing down the development of the confidence and intimacy that are necessary to the flowering of an inner life.

It is less often suspected that the confusion between the idea of divine and human fatherhood may be potentially damaging to an inner journey in people who carry a positive father image. However, vigilance is also needed here and for two precise reasons. The first is linked to memories of the Oedipus complex, which remain present and active in each of us, however our psyche may have handled it from infancy onwards.[63] These memories are accompanied by an ambivalent mixture of love and hatred, complicity and confrontation, admiration and repulsion towards the father figure, which may lead to various unconscious interferences within an inner life that is exclusively founded on this father analogy. Apart from the risk that this ambivalence may foster a certain relational instability, the most damaging interference manifests itself as an excessive sense of guilt, because of the murderous impulses towards the father, which have haunted the psyche following an aspiration to fuse with the mother.[a] The – unconscious – attempt to seek forgiveness for this then risks being projected onto the relationship with a God perceived as a father, to the point of restricting an inner life to permanent contrition made up of pious pleas ('Lord, have mercy') that do not favour the establishment of true reciprocal love. Of course, real concern not to harm another person or sadness at having hurt them is an integral part of the mystery of love. But anyone who loves – and even more so a God whose very essence is love – does not expect the loved one to wallow in incessant pleas or demands for forgiveness. He expects the loved one joyfully to welcome the love that is given and offer love in return and that both should enjoy this love fully. The second reason why a positive father image requires a certain vigilance is the risk that the representation of God from a good father experience might become the only one for the persons concerned. This widespread tendency often prevents an inner life from opening up towards other aspects

---

a   See 'Origins of the Feeling of Guilt' in Part 2 of this book.

that can characterise the presence, way of loving and desire to be loved proper to a God who is love. Spiritual experience is thereby limited the more the mental image associated with God strongly conditions the way of letting oneself be loved by him and responding to his love.

Whether we have a negative or positive father image, each of us will benefit by consciously realising that there are no objective reasons to reduce the notion of divine fatherhood to that of human fatherhood. Once stated, this distinction seems obvious, although many people have been, are and will be still in the grip of this confusion and its accompanying transference. Sigmund Freud himself founded most of his reflections on religion on the human father figure. It follows that we must distance ourselves from many of his analyses. The Jesuit André Manaranche does not hesitate to stress: 'Despite his relevant intuitions, in the Judeo-Christian context of the West, Freud was the unconscious victim of a "masculine" presentation of the Divinity. A whole aspect escaped him and his era [...] Human sciences claim to judge faith objectively, but they do not see how much their diagnosis depends on representations in which they believe. We must escape from this mirror game.'[a]

---

a   *L'Esprit et la Femme*, Paris, Seuil, 1974, p. 13.

Divine Fatherhood and Human Motherhood

Rigorous exegesis of the notion of divine fatherhood, as the Bible presents it, does not support its reduction to the fundamental characteristics of human fatherhood. The repercussions of this distinction on the mental image associated with God, and on the convictions of each of us, justify a triple clarification of the meaning of the word 'father' as applied to God. First, a clarification of the meaning of the term within the historical, inter-religious and theological context in which it first occurs in the Bible. Second, a clarification of the wider significance that the notion of divine fatherhood acquires in the Old Testament in the light of mother analogies used by certain writers and, above all, in the light of the most characteristic behaviour of this God, who wants to set up a covenant with his people. Lastly, a clarification of the meaning of the word 'father' in the mouth of Christ himself and the resulting criteria for any use of human analogies trying to be faithful to the true specificity of the gospel message.

The first clarification lies in grasping the meaning of the attribution of the word 'father' to God by setting it in its context within the theological vocabulary of the Bible. Apart from the influence of the surrounding patriarchal culture, which did not encourage the use of feminine analogies, it is important to stress the influence of the inter-religious context of the time. The attribution of the notion of father to God is not confined to the people of Israel. The term had already long been used in the beliefs of neighbouring peoples, as the exegete Joachim Jeremias recalls: 'The ancient East considers the divinity as the father of human beings, or at least some of them, and this mythical concept is widespread from earliest times [...] Clearly, in the Old Testament, the notion of God the father is linked to that of the ancient East.'[a] Paradoxically, what is specific to Israel in the use of this idea is partly the restraint with which it is used, according to the exegete Wittold Marchel: 'Although the tribes surrounding Israel usually gave their god the title of father, the Old Testament is remarkably reserved with regard to this title.'[b] This reserve remains partly characterised by a refusal to reduce the notion of divine fatherhood to the image of human biological fatherhood, as did various ancient Eastern myths, which did not hesitate to speak of 'begetting'. Joachim Jeremias picks up this point and points out another novelty essential to the understanding of the true specificity of the attribution of the word 'father' to God in the Old Testament: 'There is a fundamental difference. For the Bible, God, the creator and father, is never the ancestor or the one who begets [...] The radical novelty is that the choice of Israel as the firstborn is manifested in an historical act: the exodus from Egypt. God's fatherhood being related to a historical action profoundly modifies the notion of father.'[c] This link between the use of the word 'father' in the theological reflection of the Bible and that precise historical event – the exodus from Egypt – shows that the choice of this word does not originate from a simple analogy with the human father figure and even less from a deliberate decision to attribute a preferred sexual identity to God. 'It was not analogical reasoning that led Israel to call God its father; it was a lived experience. [...] Initially God's fatherhood was thought of in this collective historical perspective: God is revealed as Israel's father at the moment of the exodus, because he showed himself to

---

a *Abba, Jésus et son Père*, Paris, Seuil, 1972, p. 10.

b *Dieu Père dans le Nouveau Testament*, Paris, Cerf, 1966, p. 17. Joachim Jeremias says on this subject: '[The Old Testament] only rarely [fifteen times in all] uses the term "father" to designate God' (op. cit., p. 10).

c Op. cit., p. 10–11.

be its protector and feeder as well as being its master. The basic idea is that of benevolent sovereignty.'[a] This usage was not linked to any reflection on sexual identity as such. Neither did it focus on the human father image as such. It is an invitation to deepen the meaning of divine fatherhood without falling into the trap of a simplistic and reductionist identification with just the psychological attributes proper to the human father figure. This brief reframing of the Old Testament view encourages deeper consideration of the term, because the biblical writers' reserve about designating God as father also brings out their recourse to a great variety of analogies in speaking about God, his divine presence to humans or his saving action. Although with very different frequency, the analogies used are with father, mother, husband, wife, beloved, saviour, shepherd, creator, etc.[b] Moreover, to bring out the real connecting thread in the Old Testament writings, that is to say, the alliance that the God of the Bible makes with his people, the analogy of the couple, of betrothal or marriage, has pride of place. This is true both in the Wisdom literature – for example the Song of Songs or in the designation of divine Wisdom as the ideal 'bride'[c] – and in the prophetic writing, where Jeremiah, Ezechiel and Isaiah each in his turn uses the nuptial allegory[d]

---

a   *Vocabulaire de théologie biblique*, Paris, Cerf, 1988, pp. 966–967.

b   For each of these, see respectively: Ps 103:13; Is 66:13; Hos 2:21–22; Wis : 2; Ps 41:12; Wis 1:6; Is 63:8; Is 40:11; Is 45:18.

c   Wis 8:2 and 16.

d   'Yahweh says this: "I remember your faithful love, the affection of your bridal days" (Jer 2:2). "Then I saw you as I was passing. Your time had come, the time for love. [...] I gave you my oath, I made a covenant with you" – declares the Lord Yahweh – "and you became mine" (Ez 16:8). 'For your Creator is your husband, Yahweh Sabaoth is his name, the Holy One of Israel is your redeemer, he is called God of the whole world. Yes, Yahweh has called you back like a forsaken, grief-stricken wife, like the repudiated wife of his youth, says your God. I did forsake you for a brief moment, but in great compassion I shall take you back [...] No more will you be known as "Forsaken" or your country be known as "Desolation"; instead you will be called "My Delight is in her" and your country "The Wedded"; for Yahweh will take delight in you and your country will have its wedding. Like a young man marrying a virgin, your rebuilder will wed you, and as the bridegroom rejoices in his bride so will your God rejoice in you' (Is 54:5–7 and 62:4–5).

that is dear to the prophet Hosea: 'I shall betroth you to myself
for ever, I shall betroth you in uprightness and justice, in faithful
love and tenderness. Yes, I shall betroth you to myself in loyalty
and in the knowledge of Yahweh [...] When that day comes –
declares Yahweh – you will call me "My husband".'[a] This variety
of analogies lead us to conclude with Witold Marchel: 'The large
number of these images alone reveals that God's being is too rich,
too mysterious, too deep to be expressed by a single word, even
the word father.'[b]

The second clarification about the meaning of the word 'father'
attributed to God consists in considering this notion of divine
fatherhood in the light both of the mother analogies used by
some biblical authors and of the Bible God's most characteristic
behaviour. These mother analogies are not very numerous,[c] but
they are there. They were chosen despite the unfavourable cultural
and sociological context, which gives them more value and
interest. If the bare existence of these mother analogies is already
an invitation not to relate divine fatherhood only to human
fatherhood, their strong point consists in expressing a divine love
overflowing with tenderness, one that never abandons anyone:
'As a mother comforts a child, so I shall comfort you' or again:
'Can a woman forget her baby at the breast, feel no pity for the
child she has borne? Even if these were to forget, I shall not forget
you.'[d] But not content with using a few mother metaphors, the
prophetic literature has made particular use of the Hebrew term
rahamin to express the divine mercy, a term whose importance is
stressed by Christiane Méroz: 'From the same root as the word
rehem meaning the mother's womb, the term *rahamin* brings a
feminine element into the notion of divine mercy. [...] The biblical
metaphor the "womb [entrails] of mercy" has an important place.
Indeed, *rahamin* is the keyboard on which the daily hymn of the

---

a Hos 2:21–22 and 18.

b *Dieu Père dans le Nouveau Testament*, op. cit., p. 30.

c See Deut 32: 6 and 18; Num 11:11–12; Is 42:14; Is 49:15; Is 63:15; Is
   66:9–13; Jer 4:19; Jer 31:20; Hos 11:3–4; Job 38:28–29; Ps 22:11.

d Is 66:13; Is 49:15.

relation between God and his creatures is played. There is no reciprocal approach of the human being and God except through mercy, that is the key which again and again opens the door of the alliance.'[a] [64] The use of the word *rahamin* and of mother analogies faithfully sums up the most characteristic behaviour of this God who wants to make an alliance with his people, which is the story of the whole Bible. A God who, even when he is misunderstood, rejected and abandoned, continues despite everything to love his creature to the end and tirelessly opens up the way to salvation. [65] Thus his behaviour demonstrates an attitude that is more characteristic of a mother's protective instinct, as Olivier Clément points out in the homage he pays to one of the intuitions dear to Paul Evdokimov: 'Divine fatherhood seems to be reflected less in the human fatherhood of men than in the motherhood of women. Nothing in masculine nature spontaneously reproduces the religious category of fatherhood, the father instinct does not constitute a man in the way that the mother instinct constitutes a woman.'[b] This intuition has the merit of not stopping at appearances and psychological projections inherent in the evocation of divine fatherhood, in which it also perceives a reality bearing a close relation to the way of being and loving belonging to human motherhood. It reminds us of the power of certain feminine analogies also to reflect the beauty of a God who is love.

The third clarification of the meaning of the word 'father' attributed to God in the Bible consists in discerning the meaning it has when used by Christ himself. Then we can draw the consequences for the use of masculine and feminine analogies for the representation of a God of love. Of course, this discernment remains limited by the real difficulty of taking into account, on the one hand, what derives from the surrounding patriarchal culture and received religious education and, on the other, what relates to an intimate experience and a truly revealing personal journey. Calling God father cannot be considered in itself as

---

a   *Le visage maternel de Dieu*, Lausanne, Ouverture, 1989, pp. 32, 37–38.

b   'Paul Evdokimov, témoin de la beauté de Dieu' in *Contacts*, vol. XXIII, nos 73–74, 1971, p. 76.

specific to Christ's teaching, because it existed before him and even before its usage by the people of Israel. 'Leading up to the Christian era, Israel was fully aware that God is father of his people and of each of his faithful. [...] The name Father occurs frequently in rabbinical writings, where we even find the exact formulation "Our Father who art in heaven".'[a] Jesus of Nazareth received and took on the faith of his people and, consequently, everything previously revealed from the Old Testament remains the basis supporting his use of the word 'Father'. Here too this usage does not allow the reduction of the mystery of God to the pure and simple projection of psychological attributes proper to the human father figure. The reserve in the Old Testament use of the term can also be found in the synoptic Gospels. [66] Moreover, the true purpose of the dialectic between 'Father' and 'Son' – so strongly stressed in John's Gospel – is not to speculate about God's identity as father but rather to affirm Jesus of Nazareth's messianic identity, the unique bond he has with God, the knowledge of God that flows from that and which enables him to reveal God's true face. Even more precisely, it is not the word 'Father' as such, but rather the way in which Jesus uses it which reveals his intimacy with God and his messianic identity.[67] Recognition of this intimacy and this deep identity leads us to apprehend the divine reality underlying the word 'Father' from Christ's actual behaviour, in accordance with his words: 'He who has seen me has seen the Father.'[b] This very strong statement with its inseparable corollary 'My Father and I are one'[c] could not be more explicit. It makes us look to Christ's own behaviour as the source of authentic knowledge of God and not to human projections habitually raised by the notion of father: 'No one know the Father except the Son.'[d] Although Christ's attitude

---

a 'Do not imagine I have come to abolish the Law or the Prophets. I have come not to abolish but to fulfil them' Mt 5:17.

b Jn 14:9.

c Jn 10:30.

d Mt 11:27.

was not intended to abolish the Old Testament approach to this divine fatherhood,[a] it takes us over a new threshold with regard to what this approach might mean for divine love and possible intimacy with God. The Gospels unanimously testify to a Christ whose actions and words reflect a God of love who wants to be intimately close to each of us,[b] a God of love who tirelessly searches even for those farthest away from him and does not want to abandon anyone,[c] a God of love who wants to cure each one's wounds by his forgiveness constantly on offer,[d] a God of love who seeks to welcome and be welcomed,[e], a God of love who wants to be intensely loved,[f] a God of love who even when rejected and abandoned continues to forgive and to love human beings to the end.[g] All this is so true that the apostle John, considered to be his closest disciple, is not content with accounting for Christ's behaviour and message with the famous words 'God is love'[h] or by the fundamental reversal according to which 'it is not we who loved God but he who loved us [...] first'[i] or even by the liberating confidence that 'wherever our hearts condemn us, God is greater than our hearts.'[j] Above all, he also gives us this startling synthesis: 'This is what we have heard from him and are declaring to you: God is light and there is no darkness in him at all.'[k] While keeping the idea of divine fatherhood belonging to the culture and religious tradition of his time, through his life Christ shows the true identity of his 'Father', who cannot be reduced to a human

---

a   Mt 5:17.

b   See Mt 10:7; Mk 1:15; Lk 9:10; Jn 14:23.

c   See Mt 18:12–14; Mk 2:16–17; Lk 15:4–32; Jn 3:16–17.

d   See Mt 9:10–13; Mk 2:3–12; Lk 15:11–32; Jn 8:3–11.

e   See Mt 10:40; Mk 9:37; Lk 18:17; Lk 9:2–10; Jn 14:2–3 and 23.

f   See Mt 22:37–38; Mk 12:30; Lk 10:27; Jn 21:15–17.

g   See Lk 23:33–34; Jn 13:37–38 and 18:25–27 with 21:15–17.

h   1 Jn 4:8 and 16.

i   1 Jn 4:10 and 19.

j   1 Jn 3:20.

k   1 Jn 1:5.

father figure but is presented as the supreme Source of a love without 'darkness', without shadow, without any connivance with evil, who wants to invite each of us as of today[a] into a reciprocal love with him in a dimension which Christ calls 'the Kingdom of God.'[b] This is where a divine–human intimacy can take place in the depths of our being, an intimacy that can grow into eternity. The theologian Donna Singles notes that Christ presents this mysterious 'Kingdom of God'[68] through numerous analogies and that, although of course, the father analogy is one of these, Jesus does not hesitate to resort to feminine analogies to describe God's activity: 'These have a crucial place in Jesus' preaching about the Kingdom. Hence their fundamental importance for the theological question: "What God did Jesus reveal to us?" Through a woman taking yeast to make bread (Lk 13:21) or who sweeps her house to find her lost coin (Lk 15: 8–9), who anxiously awaits her time to give birth (Jn 16:21). This is 'God the mother' who shows her tenderness, her concern for the 'children born from her own womb'.[c] This takes us back to a single vital criterion for the use of feminine and masculine analogies that are in conformity with Christ's message. Rather than being driven by any cultural or psychological conditioning, their use should be guided by the absolute priority which is to disfigure as little as possible this supreme Source of a love without 'darkness' and boldly to use analogies that can make its divine beauty shine in all its dimensions. It is important to stress with Donna Singles how far careful and serene integration of feminine analogies into theological language could go hand in hand with Christ's care to eliminate the violent or vengeful aspects that some biblical writers thought good sometimes to attribute to a manly image of God.[69] They did this without realising that they were projecting a human logic like that unmasked in the second part of this book onto divine behaviour. 'It is a fact: the father

---

a   See Lk 19:5.

b   Mk 1:15.

c   'La maternité de Dieu', article published in *La Croix*, 21 December 1998.

images of God are open to a wide variety of interpretations, including anger or vengeance. On the other hand, the mother images of God always have a single theme: an overwhelming love, which never grows tired. Hence the power and richness of these analogies to renew our talk about God.'[a]

---

a Ibid.

'Though My Father and Mother Forsake Me'

Although mother analogies seem able to offer our attempts to describe divine fatherhood better ways of expressing the faith-fulness and tenderness of a God who is love, these analogies still also risk arousing psychological transferences and potentially damaging unconscious aspirations in the quest for meaning or spiritual experience. The use of the mother figure requires just as vigorous discernment as that of the father figure, because of three unconscious processes, which need to be taken into consideration so as not to fall into excessive idealisation in the use of mother analogies. We must to be careful to avoid the same mistake that may be made with father analogies: the tendency to become exclusive and not take into account the reasons why complemen-tarity between mother and father images offers better support to any theological language trying not to disfigure divine love, that is greater than anything a human being could conceive.

The first of these unconscious processes corresponds to the feminine counterpart of the most common transference in the use of the father figure. The mother figure also unconsciously reminds each of us of our own experience of a mother's presence, either a biological mother or other people who might have indirectly symbolised it. The most damaging consequences of such a transference affect most those who have a negative mother image, especially if they have had serious relationship difficulties with their biological mother. In a way that is comparable to the possible undesirable repercussions linked to the use of the father figure, there is a high chance that these people will project onto their spontaneous representation of a Mother-God certain features relative to the treatment they suffered during childhood or adolescence. This carries the same risks of spiritual paralysis linked to the rejection of a God who has become the scapegoat of a personal settling of scores or linked to a concept of God that is as illusory as it is tyrannical. Being aware of this possible transference is already a first step on the road to discernment that is careful to diminish the impact of possible disadvantages caused by the use of mother analogies, in order to get greater benefit from its advantages.[70] And this awareness also confirms the importance of not reducing theological language to a single analogy.

By contrast, the second unconscious process to be taken into account concerns those who have an eminently positive mother image. Psychology's major discoveries have established that, in the unconscious of every human being, the mother image – even of the best of mothers – remains ambivalent. From infancy onwards the mother's presence is linked to a dominating power, synonymous both with the power to satisfy desires and a humiliating dependency, that is feared, even detested.[71] Following her research into this ambivalence, psychoanalyst Janine Chasseguet-Smirgel states: 'The child of both sexes has a terrifying image in the unconscious of even the best and tenderest of mothers. This results in hostility projected onto her because of the child's lack of power.'[a] According to her, even the most harmonious mother–child relationships cannot make this ambivalence disappear: 'The child's primary lack of power, the intrinsic conditions of his or her psycho-physiological condition, the inevitable restrictions of education, mean that the image of the all-powerful good mother never repairs the image of the terrifying image of the bad mother.'[b] Being aware of this ambivalence[72] and its possible transference onto God constitutes a second stage along the

---

a   *La sexualité féminine*, Paris, Payot, 1970, p. 171.

b   Ibid, p. 171.

road of discernment, which enables us better to understand the psychological background of repression of feminine analogies in theological reflection – complicit here with patriarchal culture. Indeed, a certain resistance to giving them their complementary and reciprocal place in the evocation of the mystery of God could prove to be related to the degree of influence of the unconscious presence of this terrifying mother image. The psychoanalyst Thierry de Saussure does not hesitate to suggest: 'Perhaps the declared absence of a feminine image in the Trinitarian God [...] points defensively to such a powerful presence of the primitive mother image, that has been so repressed in the unconscious that it has been denied a stable place of complementarity and reciprocity. [...] [This repression] compensates for the unconscious desire and anxiety of the man in the face of the all-powerful image of woman.'[a] This liberating realisation could support calm and fruitful research into giving feminine analogies a truly complementary and reciprocal place within theological language.

The third unconscious process that should not be neglected here has its source in the unconscious aspiration to a fusional type of union with the mother, an aspiration that is present in each of us from birth and driven by the unconscious desire to recover the state of security and wellbeing of the mother's womb. Whatever the power of this unconscious aspiration, however strongly it is reactivated at various times during life because of anxieties or pressures linked to the outside world, psychology identifies this temptation to fuse with a state of infantile regression, which is opposed to growth characterised by interpersonal relationships in which each is aware of remaining him or herself and becoming so more and more. This distinction between fusion and communion shows what is meant by authentic love, whose flowering is not fusion, where one of the partners dissolves into the other to the point of losing their own personality. On the

---

a 'Questions psychanalytiques sur la prévalence masculine dans la religion chrétienne' in *Études théologiques et religieuses*, vol. 70(3), 1995, pp. 409–410, 416.

contrary, love is a communion, which leaves nothing to envy in the union of fusion, but respects the otherness of the other so that each partner becomes increasingly him or herself. This same fusional temptation is a risk on the spiritual level in an exclusively maternal representation of God. The unconscious desire to recover a state of fusion, analogous to that of the baby with its mother, could divert such a theological representation and lead an inner life more towards infantile regression than towards an authentic reciprocal love, in which the inalienable otherness of each can flourish.[73] Being aware of this aspiration to fuse with the mother – which is always threatening to resurface – constitutes a third stage along the road to discernment that enables us to grasp the importance of completing these mother analogies with father analogies. Just as the presence and role of the father are thought to prevent this fusional union with the mother and promote the child's harmonious growth, a theological language that takes care to use both father and mother analogies could contribute more to spiritual growth, in which each of us of us, in our relation with God, was aware of becoming what we are ourselves in the depths of our being, as well as learning little by little to take on our appropriate role with maturity and responsibility.

Although that image of a child's development benefiting from mother and father love that are both present also has limits and disadvantages – like any image – nevertheless it prevents any of these three unconscious processes, inherent in the use of mother analogies, from keeping these analogies out of theological language.[74] Reverting to these unconscious processes is the more widespread because it is driven by a self-defence mechanism, a justification for our own religious education, often marked by a confusion between the notion of divine fatherhood and the fundamental characteristics of human fatherhood. This strengthens the tendency to repress or underestimate the dangers in the use of the father image, among which impressions of distance, absence, harshness, and severity are not the least. Even when it is freed from the unconscious reduction of divine fatherhood to attributes linked to the human father figure, the exercise of this discernment requires care to compensate for the exclusive use of father or mother analogies. It must draw on both human father and mother love, while qualitatively going beyond them: 'Though my father and mother forsake me, God will gather me up!'[a] The psalmist's confidence and hope sum up all the discernment criteria we have previously set out: a mysterious divine–human correspondence in love that allows recourse to father and mother analogies without thereby reducing the mystery of a God who transcends them; vigilance not to remain prisoner of certain cultural and psychological conditioning; and above all great care not to disfigure divine tenderness that cannot be set on the same level as human love, which is sometime disfigured by evil.[75] Thus the psalmist compares the tenderness of this God of love to 'the tenderness of a father for his children'[b] and that felt by 'a little child in its mother's arms'.[c] Finally, he ends up seeing tenderness not as just one attribute of God among others but as the heart of the divine essence itself: 'God is tenderness.'[d]

---

a   Ps 27:10.

b   Ps 103:13.

c   Ps 131:2.

d   Ps 103:8; 111:4; 116:5; 145:8.

'More Beautiful than the Sun'

Under the yoke of theological representations driven by a particular surrounding culture, a particular religious education or a difficulty in believing themselves worthy of being loved, many people – believers or not – have been unable to envisage this divine tenderness, with all the consequences that inability entails for their inner livers, their personal convictions, even their interest in the question of God. Although the inclusion of mother analogies invites us to take this misunderstood aspect more into consideration, nevertheless it still risks creating a difficulty in accessing another analogy that is also apt for expressing this mysterious correspondence between a feminine way of loving and that of a God who is love: the analogy not of the mother but of woman as such. Certainly, repression of this analogy remains fundamentally linked to the influence of patriarchal culture, to ignorance of the psychic importance of sexual identity and the perception from infancy of the mother's terrifying omnipotence, which drives the psyche to repress any feminine imagery in general, whether maternal or other. However, with the image of woman this process of repression also derives from psychic ambivalence towards the mother image, an ambivalence characterised by the coexistence of a desired distance in reaction to the negative mother image and the desired attachment in reaction to her positive image. In fact, unconscious attachment to the mother, more or less active according to the psychic development of the subject, may limit a man's capacity to give a place to another woman in his heart or thoughts. Within the masculine psyche this attachment not only derives from the fusional desire we have already discussed, but also from the loving desire inherent in the Oedipus complex that is never finally resolved. It is very probable that this unconscious process also contributed to the notable inability to give other feminine analogies a place in a certain kind of theological reflection, which has been pursued mainly by men potentially exposed to this unconscious influence. Becoming aware of this, means we take care to prevent this process from profiting – as it seems to have done with the development of the cult of Mary – from a successful integration of mother analogies into religious language that, paradoxically, fosters the repression of analogies relative to woman and her mystery. This vigilance constitutes another challenge to be faced by any quest for feminine and masculine analogies best fitted to express the many aspects of divine love.

Meeting this challenge means that we no longer represent God's mystery only by father and mother analogies. We widen our search to other masculine and feminine analogies, which can limit the possible risks of an infantilising spirituality.[76] One of the principal obstacles to this broader approach comes from the fact that many people, including Christians, think of God in terms of a vague deism, around which the associated ideas are often reduced to those of Creator, the Origin par excellence, and therefore evoke only parental figures, particularly that of the father. However, in Christian revelation the mystery of this God of love is not confined to a simple theism but finds its ultimate expression in the mystery of the Trinity, confessing the existence in God himself of movements of love, of divine persons[77] who love each other so intensely that this results in total unity[78] in respected otherness.[79] The mystery of the Trinity takes all of us back to our own experience of love – what link can we envisage between love and the very essence of a divine mystery if that mystery was just solitude in itself?[80] It also invites humans to join in this divine love, finally to enter into a unique loving relationship with each of the divine Persons concerned. In Christian tradition, these are called 'Father', 'Son' and 'Holy Spirit'.[81] This unique relationship enables us to glimpse the appropriateness of the mystery of the

Trinity to express the depth and beauty of the divine Being, of whom the Old Testament writers had a premonition when they used analogies as various as that of father, mother, husband, wife, friend. In the Trinity, every aspect of the mystery of love comes alive and realisable in God, with God.

These different aspects call upon us to rediscover the depths of this Trinitarian mystery, in which the supreme Source of love is revealed. For the Person of the 'Father' analogical language that takes care to include both maternal and paternal tenderness has already been suggested, in order to perceive the beauties of his love more deeply. As for the Person of the 'Son', Christian tradition uses analogies whose diversity and complementarity are difficult to surpass, since they refer to the strongest and most beautiful bonds of love that exist here below. Christ is regularly compared to a friend,[a] an older brother[b] or a bridegroom.[c] [82] The last image, which takes on all the symbolism of betrothal and marriage dear to the prophetic writings and which Christ applies to himself, has become the chief analogical reference of Christian mysticism, particularly through many commentaries on the Song of Songs. By way of contrast, for the Person of the 'Holy Spirit' the most abstract analogical language has been used, which has driven many believers, including professional theologians to call him an 'unknown God', according to the expression chosen by Victor Dillard to express this frustration. He invites us to overcome it in order to discover 'an attractive person with all his impenetrable mystery and fascinating shine'.[d][83] Of the three divine Persons, the Holy Spirit is the one for whom the use of feminine

---

a 'I shall no longer call you servants, because a servant does not know his master's business; I call you friends, because I have made known to you everything I have learnt from my Father' (Jn 15:15).

b 'We are well aware that God works with those who love him, those who have been called in accordance with his purpose, and turns everything to their good. He decided beforehand who were the ones destined to be moulded to the pattern of his Son, so that he should be the eldest of many brothers' (Rom 8: 28–29).

c See Mt 9:15 and 25:1–10; Mk 2:19; Lk 5:34; Jn 3:28–29.

d *Au dieu inconnu, Paris*, Beauchesne, 1938, p. 9.

analogies would be the most appropriate. According to the Bible, he is the Person who gives life, spiritually gives birth, inspires, consoles, comforts.[a] This is a whole way of being and loving[84] which, of course is not exclusive to women here below,[85] but is nevertheless, fundamentally feminine.[86] This aspect of the Spirit's mystery did not escape the Dominican Yves Congar and even led him to state: 'Particularly in the Church – but it is also true of society – a pre-Trinitarian monotheism [where the "Father" alone is counted], or a *de facto* "Christomonism" [where Christ alone comes counted], in short, a certain forgetfulness of the Holy Spirit and pneumatology [from the Greek word *pneuma* meaning "breath" or "spirit"] led to the establishment of a patriarchal type and the dominance of the masculine.'[b] In addition to the repression of a feminine dimension for all the reasons already mentioned, it is indeed a 'certain forgetfulness' of the Holy Spirit that constitutes one of the major pitfalls of much theology. As well as this, such theology often has a tendency to reify the Spirit, failing to recognise the Spirit's personal dimension and the way of loving that entails. Pointing out these two pitfalls will allow us to illustrate again how a healthy integration of feminine analogies is possible in the evocation of this Trinitarian God, and also that this integration supports the discovery and acceptance of neglected aspects of divine love that is even greater than many believers or non-believers might suspect.

These two pitfalls of forgetfulness and reification of the Holy Spirit have been fostered by many theological tendencies, which need to be identified in order to weaken their influence. If the 'pre-Trinitarian monotheism' mentioned by Yves Congar, in which only God the Father is taken into account, indirectly relates back to the tendency to deism previously mentioned, 'Christomonism' relates indirectly to the tendency only to refer systematically to the figure of Christ. The development of such tendencies has made it very difficult to attain a balanced view of the mystery of

---

a   See respectively Jn 6:63; Jn 3:5–8; Lk 3:5–8; Lk 12:11–12; Jn 14:16–18; Jn 16:12–13.

b   *Je crois en l'Esprit Saint*, op. cit., p. 729.

the Trinity in which, according to the Creed, the Holy Spirit is 'together worshipped and glorified'.[87] The complementarity and reciprocity of the Son and the Holy Spirit, asserted throughout scripture,[88] have probably also suffered from an almost exclusive insistence on the bond between the Persons of the Father and the Son – the Holy Spirit then being reduced to their bond of love[89] – so that some people have sometimes had the impression that it was more a question of a Binity than a true Trinity.[90] Another difficulty has often been added to that of giving the Person of the Holy Spirit its place. On the one hand, there is the linguistic ambiguity of the word 'spirit; which does not immediately make us think of a person and, on the other, there are biblical passages that are not very explicit and do not support the recognition of this personal dimension – a dimension affirmed by the very nature of the activities that Christ attributes to him (her).[91] Moreover, there is also a tendency to identify the Holy Spirit with the simple presence of Christ, actualised and universalised in the human heart.[92] Behind that tendency lies a modern version of modalism, the train of thought during the early centuries of the Christian era which refused to count three divine Persons and regarded these as three different modes of presence of one and the same divine Person.[93] Lastly, the tendency only to refer to a purely functional role of the Holy Spirit within salvation history has also not helped people to meditate on this Spirit's way of being and loving within an interpersonal relationship.[94] If we step back from the theological conditioning constituted by these many tendencies, this gives us an inner space without which no further deepening can take place, or any new viewpoint be envisaged.

More and more theologians, men and now women,[95] are inviting us to deepen the personal and feminine dimension of the Holy Spirit, starting from its close relation with the mysterious biblical figure of divine Wisdom.[96] Rather than being reduced to a divine attribute, in several Old Testament books, Wisdom gradually comes to correspond with the person and intimate presence of God to humans,[97] with a double originality. Not only is she presented in feminine form[98] – rarer for evoking God's presence – but she is not confined to a mother

role and recovers many feminine analogies which are even more
rarely applied to God, particularly 'woman friend,'[a] 'sister'[b] and
(especially) 'bride.'[c] [99] The exegete Pierre-Emile Bonnard stresses
the novelty of the bride analogy, involving the opposite of the
role of bridegroom usually attributed to God by the prophetic
writings: 'Wisdom stands before humans as an irreproachable,
attractive, generous and ennobling companion, capable of living
in perfect harmony with the one she first loves and who loves
her in return [cf. Prov 4:6–9; Sir 15:2b; 51:19 in Hebrew; Wis
8:2–9]. The marriage between divine Wisdom and humanity, her
bridegroom, thus celebrates in a new key the marriage sung from
Hosea onwards of Yahweh God and the nation of Israel, his
bride.'[d] The Dominican Philippe Lefebvre stresses the loving quest
and passion that Wisdom arouses: '[Wisdom] is not an inaccessible divinity that has fortuitously appeared, and vanishes all too
soon. She is a sweet and certain presence, who has already been
given when she is sought. Wisdom was there like a mother and
I did not know it! She is also the bride whom the wise man is
allowed to know: "Hold her close, and she will make you great"
(Prov 4:8). [...] Indeed love alone is the proper bond with her.
She cannot be stored up but must be pursued in a loving quest.
Wisdom proclaims: "I love those who love me; whoever searches
eagerly for me finds me (Prov 8:17). Passionately desired like a
bride, Wisdom compels her lover to declare himself, to express
the desire of his heart.'[e]

These analogies invite us to meditate and to welcome these
neglected aspects of the biblical God's way of being and loving.
They also throw light on the Holy Spirit's way of being and
loving, when we take into consideration his (her) close relation to

---

a 'Wisdom is a spirit friendly to humanity' (Wis 1:6).

b 'Say to Wisdom, "You are my sister!"' (Prov 7:4).

c 'Wisdom I loved and searched for from my youth; I resolved to have her as my
   bride, I fell in love with her beauty' (Wis 8: 2).

d *La Sagesse en Personne*, Paris, Cerf, 1966, p. 118.

e 'La Sagesse: rencontre de l'homme et de la femme' in *La vie spirituelle*, no.
   731, June 1999, p. 205.

Wisdom. The exegete Claude Larcher explains this close relation by making the following points: 'The two realities are identified in several ways. Wisdom has a spirit (Wis 7:22b), or she is a spirit (1:6), she acts in the form of a spirit (7:7b). Moreover she has power and in the Old Testament the various functions of the Spirit are attributed to her. She exercises a universal cosmic role, she arouses prophets, she becomes humanity's guide, then that of the chosen people. Lastly, she appears as the inner master of souls. The assimilation applies to so many points at once that Wisdom appears as a sublimation of the part played by the Spirit in the Old Testament.'[a] [100] Yves Congar clarifies the possible contribution of wisdom to a theology of the Holy Spirit with respect to personalisation and feminisation: 'The Wisdom literature of Hellenised Judaism contains a remarkable reflection on Wisdom, which comes close enough to the Spirit almost to identify the two realities, at least if one considers them in action. [...] Two values must be stressed, which are of interest to a further theology of the Holy Spirit. First, a certain personalisation of the Spirit. In the case of Wisdom this is progressively affirmed from Proverbs 8:22–31. [...] Sometimes the personalisation is merely a literary expression. However, the rigorous monotheism of the Jewish religion associated realities with God, which were God, but which in God represented modes of action, presence, being (with humans): Shekinah and Wisdom. What is said about her in Wisdom chapters 8 and 9 expresses the intimate action of the Spirit of God and is applicable to the Spirit. [...] Like Shekinah, Wisdom [...] is a feminine reality. She is loved and sought like a woman (Sir 14:22f). She is bride and mother (14:26f; 15:2f). She is the source of fertility, intimacy, peaceful joy. [...] In Christian reflection the feminine character of God is finally attributed to the Holy Spirit.'[b]

Perhaps 'attributed' is saying a lot, if we take into account the cultural reticence and psychological repression to which feminine analogies in theological language have continually

---

a   *Études sue le livre de la Sagesse*, Paris, J. Gabalda and Co., 1969, p. 411.

b   *Je crois en l'Esprit Saint*, op. cit., pp. 28, 30, 723, 724.

been subjected. However, it seems that as well as using feminine symbols like water and the dove,[101] the first centuries saw the birth of theological approaches susceptible to this feminine way of being belonging to the Holy Spirit. This occurred as soon as Judeo-Christian circles developed. The Jesuit Jean Daniélou, an expert in Judeo-Christian theology, finds within it an undeniable attachment to this dimension of the mystery of the Spirit. Among others, he cites the experience of one of the great spiritual figure in heterodox Judeo-Christianity, one called Elxai: 'Elxai had received a book in a vision. This book had been given to him by an angel. This angel was huge, 96 miles high: "He was accompanied by a feminine being whose dimensions were the same as we have said. The masculine being was the Son of God and the feminine being was called the Holy Spirit" (Elench IX, 13). [...] Here we find ourselves directly in the context of Judeo-Christian spirituality, in the company of the *Gospel of Peter* or the *Shepherd*. Indeed we have already met most of the features that are found here: the gigantic size of the angels, the Son of God and the Holy Spirit seen in the form of two angels, the feminine character of the Spirit.'[a] In the *Odes of Solomon*, whose composition can be set between the end of the first century and the beginning of the second century, and in which the Holy Spirit has pride of place, the Dominican Dominique Cerbelaud notes an attribution of feminine and maternal analogies to the Holy Spirit and to the Father: 'It is very possible that here we see the beginnings of a very archaic "theo-lyricism", which the massive canonisation of masculine images later completely repressed, to the point that they were forgotten. Thus the Trinity has two feminine persons: the Father, who despite this designation possesses all the attributes of a mother; and the Holy Spirit, who appears as a sort of "midwife" [...] As for the Spirit, we know that the Semitic languages, and in particular Syriac, spoke of it in the feminine. The fluidity of this figure, its "intuitive" aspect (both inward and "abroad"): all this contributes to reinforcing this feminine polarity [...] The question of the "feminine in God"

---

a   *Théologie du judéo-christianisme*, Paris, Desclée de Brouwer, 1958, p. 77.

keeps coming back, revived today by the discussions of the institutional functioning of the Church. Hasn't the time now come to try also to reintegrate this aspect of the mystery into theological discourse? In this context the *Odes of Solomon* and other very ancient texts of our tradition could turn out to be surprisingly modern.'[a] Olivier Clément also points out a similar sensibility within a reflection on the diaconate belonging to the Christian tradition of the third century: 'The Didascalia [of the apostles] gives a very important precision: "The deacon has the place of Christ and you must love him. You must honour the deaconesses in place of the Holy Spirit." This statement clearly sums up the tradition: man is ontically linked to the Word, woman to the Holy Spirit.'[b]

As Dominique Cerbelaud stresses, these theological sensibilities ended up being forgotten, thanks to the 'massive canonisation of masculine images'. This occurred, among other reasons, because of the prolonging of patriarchal influence, which led to the exclusive use of masculine analogies, including calling the Person of the Holy Spirit 'he'.[102] But the existence of these sensibilities at least has the merit of illustrating, on the one hand, that the integration of feminine analogies into theological language is possible and, on the other, that among the rare suggestions truly compatible with a balanced Trinitarian faith[103], the one which invites us to take more notice of the use of feminine analogies for the Holy Spirit can claim to have the best foundation, in the Bible as in Christian tradition. Moreover, Christian tradition has always recognised in the Holy Spirit 'the hypostasis of Beauty', according to the expression of Serge Boulgakov[c] for whom: 'The Holy Spirit has the invincible force of Beauty.'[d] Paul Evdokimov also insists on this conviction, whose presence he notes in the thought of Fyodor Dostoyevsky: 'The Third Person of the Trinity

---

a   'Un Dieu d'eau et de vent, l'Esprit Saint dans les Odes de Salamon' in *La vie spirituelle*, no. 710, May–June, 1994, pp. 317–319.

b   'Paul Evdokimov, témoin de la beauté de Dieu' in *Contacts*, op. cit., p. 76.

c   *La Paraclet*, Paris, Aubier, 1946, p. 194.

d   Ibid, p. 269.

is revealed as the Spirit of Beauty. Dostoyevsky understood that well: "The Holy Spirit, he says, is the direct seizure of Beauty".'[a] According to the Bible, this divine Beauty belongs precisely to Wisdom, in whom holy scripture invites us to recognise 'the very source of beauty', reflected through so many human experiences of beauty – inward and well as outward – in the contemplation of the world, and with feminine beauty taking pride of place: [104] "If, charmed by their beauty, they have taken these for gods, let them know how much the Master of these excels them, since it was the very source of beauty that created them".'[b] This drives Solomon to exclaim: '[Wisdom] is more beautiful than the sun, she outshines all the constellations; [...] I resolved to have her as my bride, I fell in love with her beauty.'[c]

---

a   *L'art de l'icône, théologie de la beauté,* Paris, Desclée de Brouwer, 1972, p. 12.

b   Wis 13:3.

c   Wis 7:29; 8:2.

Towards Divine–Human Intimacy

If we remain vigilant about the largely unconscious influence of various kinds of cultural, psychological and sometimes theological conditioning that have prevented consideration of these neglected as aspects of a God who is tenderness, this will gives us the means to discover or rediscover the source and the ultimate, transcendent expression of many aspects of the mystery of love in the Christian mystery of the Trinity: the love of a father, mother, husband, wife, brother, sister and friend[a] become possible analogies and even indirect reflections here below of a divine love that is even greater than human beings dare to believe.[105] If each aspect of the mystery of love is revealed as alive and realisable in God, with God, that theological representation challenges people who think of themselves as non-believers, as well as those who have already consciously embarked upon an inner life. For the former it is a matter of questioning themselves differently, no longer taking up a stand towards a reductionist representation of God that has sometimes been inculcated since childhood or maintained by caricatures drawn from their cultural environment. For the latter it is, above all, a question of not preventing such a God from leading them even further along the road of intimacy with himself, offering them his divine love under the aspect and in the

---

a See for each of these aspects, see respectively Ps 103:13; Is 66:13; Hos 2:21–22; Wis 8:2 and 16; Heb 2:11–18; Prov 7:4; Jn 15:15; Wis 1:6.

way that he judges to be most appropriate, on grounds that he alone knows deeply (their personal history, their secret wounds, their psychological profile, their sensitivity, their own way of being and loving, their sexual identity etc.).[106] This shows one of the main reasons why entering a spiritual life cannot be identified with a form of infantilism, as some psychoanalytic trends have sometimes made out, when these are impregnated with a representation of God reduced to divine fatherhood, often confused with psychological aspects belonging to human fatherhood. On the contrary, the personal relationship that can be formed with the 'Father', but also, to take a parallelism dear to St Irenaus of Lyons with the 'Word-Son' and 'Wisdom-Spirit'[a] [107] is more like engaging in spiritually and psychologically reciprocal love.

The Song of Songs remains the boldest and most powerful scriptural expression of it. This love song, charged with eroticism, originally composed to celebrate the love between a man and a woman, did not get into the Bible by chance and has a very special symbolic weight. Indeed, the Bible is, above all, intended as the place where the mystery of God is revealed, his covenant with his people and also with each human being, the mystery of earthly life and its ultimate meaning. While remaining a homage to the greatness and beauty of human love, the Song of Songs leads to the deepest of these three mysteries: God's deepest identity as mystery of love himself constituted by intra-divine movements of love,[108] to which human beings are invited;[b] the deepest identity of God's covenant with his people and then with each human being in reciprocal divine–human love;[c] the deepest identity of earthly

---

a   'Indeed there has always been in [God] Word and Wisdom, the Son and the Spirit' (*Contre les hérésies* [Against Heresies] book IV, chapter 20, para 1, Paris, Cerf, 1965, p. 627; see also parallel texts: II, 30, 9; III, 24, 2 and IV 17 4.

b   'God is love' (1 Jn 4:8 and 16) and 'I have made your name known to them and will continue to make it known, so that the love with which you loved me may be in them, and so that I may be in them' (Jn 17:26).

c   'You must love the Lord your God with all your heart, with all your soul, and with all your mind' (Mt 22:37) and 'I have loved you just as the Father has loved me. Remain in my love. [...] Remain in me as I in you' (Jn 15:9 and 4).

life as a continual apprenticeship in love with the prospect of living into eternity in the intensest possible reciprocal love with God.[a] The poem itself does not favour this or that allegorical key to interpret it. This poem of absolute love does not exclude any of these dimensions and thus embraces them all. In order to illustrate this theme of reciprocal divine–human love, Christian mystical tradition has produced many commentaries,[109] which attribute the man's role to God, in particular, to Christ and the woman's role to humanity and, in particular, the individual human soul. In the Song of Songs, the woman's search for her beloved is thus compared to different stages of a spiritual life bent on achieving total union with God. This description reaches heights of discernment and spiritual insight in St John of the Cross. The absence of an allegorical key allows those who are no longer dependent on an exclusively masculine representation of God to identify the woman in poem with divine Wisdom, even more so because the Song of Songs forms part of the Wisdom literature – where the divine Presence is represented by Wisdom – and not the prophetic writings where God is regularly compared to a husband. Moreover, the composition of the Song is symbolically attributed to Solomon, as is the book of Wisdom where the divine Presence is described as an ideal bride: 'The marriage union of divine Wisdom with man, her husband, celebrates in a new key the marriage proclaimed from Hosea onwards between Yahweh God and the nation of Israel, his bride.'[b] [110] This interpretation also has the merit, among others, of being in line with a biblical history where it is not usually the human being who goes in search of God, but rather God, who even when he is misunderstood and rejected, tirelessly tries to unite with humans who flee from him, offering them his love again and inviting them to welcome it.[111] Although

---

a   'God chose us in Christ before the world was made to be holy and faultless before him in love' (Eph 1:4) and 'For I am convinced that neither death nor life [...] nor things present, nor things to come [...] nor anything else in all creation will be able to separate us from the love of God in Christ Jesus' (Rom 8:38 and 39).

b   Pierre-Émile Bonnard, *La Sagesse en Personne*, op. cit., p. 118.

it is true that none of the main possible interpretations of the Song of Songs can claim to correspond at all points with its content in a fully coherent way, nevertheless, these different approaches are not contradictory. They pay glowing homage to its symbolic power linking the many aspects of the mystery of love to their fulfilment in divine–human intimacy. Christian mysticism sees in it the ultimate meaning of the words and acts of love here below as a continual apprenticeship in love with the prospect one day of the most intense and beautiful union with God. That intensity and that beauty are inseparable from a divine tenderness which, when we have been freed from certain cultural and psychological forms of conditioning, will appear even greater, beyond anything that humans dare to hope.

Epilogue
Divine–Human Loves

The Ultimate Meaning of Love, the Ultimate Meaning of Life

Anyone who has experienced, even just once in their lifetime, the wonder of true love will not be astonished that the Song of Songs touches countless people, whether they are believers or not. Through their own experience of love, they have glimpsed a reality that transcends all the other dimensions of their life and cannot be reduced to mere biological attraction, or set within an exclusively materialist vision of human existence.[112] 'True love, which has something of the eternally adolescent about it [...] often constitutes a "raw" spiritual experience, the glimpse of unity in difference, passionate desire for the other to exist and exist beyond death,' remarks Olivier Clément,[a] as if two people truly in love found themselves, often unwittingly, in communion with the absolute: 'If the Song of Songs is a love song – of affectionate and erotic love – which symbolises the union of God and the soul, that is because human love, both affectionate and erotic, has something to do with God. For many it remains one of the only mystical experiences they are given here below. [...] Many lives [...] might grasp, in the light of a theological exploration of the passion of love, that they have been devoted, perhaps by that

---

a *Corps de mort et de gloire*, op. cit., pp 83–84.

very passion, to a quest for the Absolute. The truly spiritual know and respect this.'[a] [113]

Closer even than the link between the mystery of love and that of God, Christian mysticism sees in the Song of Songs the symbol of this reciprocal divine–human love, in which the ultimate meaning of love here below is revealed and, finally, the ultimate meaning of life. In its eyes, all creation, all evolution from the beginning of the Universe has been willed and guided towards the progressive emergence of a living being endowed with a consciousness capable of learning to love, so that it can one day live in reciprocal love with God. From this viewpoint, the ultimate meaning of life for humans consists in learning to love, to develop our capacity to offer and accept love, with a view to experiencing the most intense and beautiful possible union with God. Whether in life as a couple, a parental relationship, a sibling bond, a friendship or any other interpersonal relationship, every act and every word of love given or received in daily life acquires an immense value. They reinforce in ourselves or in those round us, the confidence in being loved and the power to love which, for each of us, will have repercussions on our present happiness and our own present or future relationship with God.

This link between human love and divine–human love experienced by each heart, such as it has become, this link between the happiness we can give today to those dear to us and their happiness to come in God in eternity,[114] constitutes one of the most precious gifts that Christian mysticism can offer any genuine love and, in particular, to life as a couple. Not only does the link enable the unification between daily life and a spiritual quest, in particular, a reconciliation between erotic passion and mystical aspiration, but it also gives life and love a sufficiently lofty meaning[115] for anyone to draw from it a strong motivation[116] capable of sustaining the natural impetus, which, on its own, might not keep love going over the long term, much less intensify it. That meaning and motivation encourage the inner renewal of what is truly essential, a renewal without which even the most

---

a   Ibid, pp. 79, 84.

blooming love would fade over time. If we grasp this ultimate meaning of love, we will give ourselves the means to renew day after day in concrete situations the serious and magnificent choice we have made to promote the happiness of the one we love. Inner communing on the immense value of each word and act of love makes us careful before we return to the presence of the other.[117] We should regularly ask the two most important questions relevant to keeping alive the priority of constantly assuring the one we love about the love being given: 'What word or action will contribute most to increase his or her confidence in being truly loved?' 'What word or action will contribute most to increase his or her capacity to love and mine?' This daily questioning as an inner leitmotiv, pursued reciprocally,[118] will transfigure time. Then that enemy synonymous with the fading of love will be transformed into a true ally. It will allow for this continual renewal of what is essential,[119] which is only possible over the long term. It becomes the gift offered to a reciprocal love so that day after day, it attains its highest degree of intensity.

If Christian mysticism, fed by the Song of Songs, invites us to see in human love – truly lived and constantly renewed – a remarkable preparation for the reciprocal divine–human love, for which each of us was created, it also invites us to discover the support that the development of an inner life can give to that human love. The chief foundation of this support remains inseparable from the deep nature of an inner life, which consists in having a loving relationship with God and thus being linked to a supplementary source of love here below – and not just any source. This is the supreme Source of love, better placed than anyone else to initiate an inner healing of each one's secret wounds, to meet our most intimate aspirations and touch the depths of our being, where no one else has been. If we welcome this divine love, and are able to confide in God when facing this or that disappointment, we will know where to rest our hearts when a calm conversation is not yet possible with our partner and thus not allow an inner uneasiness grow into a 'timebomb', which will not pick the right tone or the right moment for finding mutual understanding. That mutual understanding will also be encouraged by the discovery and welcoming of a God of love, who wishes to heal our secret wounds and invites each of us to look kindly on our own personal wounds and those that might have driven our partner to react negatively.[120]

Through the development of an inner life, this mutual understanding could also turn a corner on the voyage to discover the mystery of the human heart – your own heart and the heart of the one you love – because if you are living in reciprocal divine–human love you are constantly reminded that each of our hearts has been created, ultimately to enjoy infinite love with God. Once we realise that the intensity of our desire to be loved and to love has its origin and deepest reason there, once we realise that only this God of love can one day respond fully to our desire, then we become capable of coping in a more positive and dynamic way with the inevitable gap between everyday reality and the ideal of love each of us carries within us. That constructive coping enables us to become partly reconciled with the existence of such a gap, as well as with the feelings of lack and loneliness inherent in the life of any couple, even the closest. This state remains fundamentally linked to the greatness of the mystery of each of us in our ultimate destiny, which is inseparable from an infinite love that is not of this world. Realising this will also help us to grasp that the true perspective is not to attain that ideal here below, but to try to approach it through the weaknesses and limitations inherent in the human condition, as well as learning to rejoice in every advance along the road of mutual growth in love, however insignificant and ordinary it may appear. Indeed, the smallest advance has great value in God's eyes. As Creator, he is well placed to know the complexity of the parameters and the many obstacles standing in the way of this common apprenticeship in love.[121] Finally, knowledge of the ultimate reason for this inevitable gap between everyday reality and the ideal of love, which each of us carries within us, not only makes constructive coping possible but invites us to redouble our attention to the desire to be loved in our partner's heart. When we realise the presence of that thirst for absolute, infinite, divine love in each of us, this becomes a passionate appeal never to underestimate the presence and power of this desire to be loved, even in those who permanently hide it behind an assumed front. When we realise more fully how much the human heart constantly needs to be reassured about the love offered to it, we learn not to neglect loving words which can be spoken. We learn not to neglect body language – particularly its erotic momentum – loving gestures which can create confidence in being loved.[122] We understand, finally, that each loving word and gesture deserves to be enjoyed to the last breath.[123] It is not only for the present happiness of each but in view of their happiness to come with God, who only asks to love intensely and be intensely loved by the human heart, such as it has become.

Christian mysticism invites each of us, whatever our state of life or our past, to enter this reciprocal divine–human love, as of today, with our heart just as it is. And as a notable feature in the spiritual history of humanity, it has also developed states of life, such as vocations called 'religious', where this reciprocal love with God not only takes first place but an exclusive place. Here the link between human love and divine–human love in the symbolism of the Song of Songs again proves enlightening to correct many prejudices about such states of life. The link reveals that the monastic vocation – to cite only this most radical form – has two absolutely fundamental points in common with the vocation of marriage. First, it is also characterised by a reciprocal love, in which the monk takes seriously this continual divine Presence and inwardly prepares to welcome this love and to love it in return with all the fibres of his being. Second, the challenge of everyday renewal of the essential, notably his confidence in being loved and his power of loving, is also vital, to allow intimacy with God to last over the long term and to tend, day after day, towards its highest degree of intensity. The main source of fulfilment and happiness is also to be found in the degree of confidence reached, both in the conviction of being truly loved and the conviction of being able to make the one you love intimately happy.

That degree of confidence may even reach great heights within a monastic vocation when this relies daily on two secret aids to the possible flowering of divine human love. The first is constantly to remember that this divine Presence can offer infinite love at any moment, because it is the supreme Source of love. Because it created human beings and taught them to love, this Source is able to offer love of a quality even greater than the most loving people here below. The second aid is constantly to remember that, because this divine Presence is capable of plumbing the depths of the human heart and therefore knowing what is in it, it is able to welcome the love this heart offers it in all its intensity. That last point needs to be duly stressed, because perhaps there is no greater happiness for one who loves than to be intimately convinced that the loved one knows how great this love is.[124] Likewise, there is probably no greater encouragement to always loving more than to know how well your love is known, recognised, understood, welcomed and enjoyed by the person you love. Moreover, being fully aware that God's heart also desires to be intensely loved,[a] being aware that no one is more receptive to signs of love than the very Source of love and being aware that knowing such signs of love are very rare, even in many religious practices, increases the monk's happiness in knowing that this mysterious divine presence knows the intensity of the love being offered.

Anyone who takes account of the presence in God himself of this desire to be intensely loved by human beings, without forgetting his desire also to love humans intensely, will be able to glimpse the specific beauty of a monastic vocation and the particular repercussions this specificity entails in the intimacy of a reciprocal divine–human love. God's yearning to be loved cannot be felt and expressed in the same way by someone who already enjoys strong love in a human relationship and by someone who expects everything from God alone. And God's yearning to love cannot be felt and expressed in the same way by someone who is already offering his or her most intimate mystery to another human being and someone who offers it to God alone.[125] Confidence in the correspondence between human and divine ways of expecting and offering love,[b] confidence in God's ardent desire to be loved,

---

a See 'A God who Wants to be Loved' in Part 3 of this book.

b See 'I am Wonderfully Made, Wonderful are your Works' in Part 3 of this book.

confidence in the capacity of this divine Presence to know to the full the love it is being offered, become for the monk motivations and appeals to engage his humanity, his sensitivity, his affection, his sexual identity, his way of expecting and offering love as fully as possible in a reciprocal love with God.[126] Then his whole being, including his most intimate yearning to love and be loved can become transfigured into a language of love addressed to God, in which the strong impetus called 'Eros' can flower.[127] 'Eros' dwells in every human being and its powerful presence indirectly reveals his true identity and ultimate destiny.[128] 'We must love with all the force of Eros', writes Olivier Clément. 'St John Climacus said that we should love God as we love a fiancée, a wife. Burning with this love, the monk becomes "an apostolic man". He has the right to speak of God because he knows him with his whole being. He will not speak of God like a theologian in books but like one of whom it can be said that "having pure prayer he is truly a theologian". When he speaks of God he is a traveller telling tales. [...] It is silly, we squabble about God's existence. It would be better to listen carefully to those who know him from experience. We see that the faith and total knowledge this experience gives do not degrade their humanity but magnify it.'[a]

Celebrating divine–human love in a way that shows the greatness of human love and its mysterious correspondence with divine love, the symbolism of the Song of Songs reveals the ultimate meaning of human existence in the light of God's love, imperfectly known and so often disfigured by psychological projections at work in each of us. The identification of these partly unconscious processes should have enabled us no longer to remain dependent on widespread spontaneous representations of God. Above all, it has invited us to glimpse, discover or rediscover the love imperfectly known of a God, who does not want or permit evil, a God who wants to heal the secret wounds of the human heart, a God who invites each of us to enter, as of now, a reciprocal love with him, a God who only asks to shower upon human beings the many aspects of his divine tenderness, so as to lead this reciprocal divine–human love to its highest degree of intensity.

---

a *Questions sur l'homme*, Paris, Stock, 1972, pp. 98–99.

Notes

1 The refusal to associate notions of divine love and omnipotence would certainly be understandable and highly laudable if it were trying to say that love would not be love if it acted in a domineering, crushing way. But isn't that representation of omnipotence still too dependent on the projection discussed here to see that another meaning could be given to omnipotence, a meaning that no longer misrepresented the nature of love?

2 In his spiritual writings, full of mystical sensibility, Maurice Zundel says that the true origin of the indignation in the face of evil felt by human beings lies in the extreme, even infinite opposition between the slightest form of evil and the existence of this God of love. He sees this as the reason for the strange feeling about certain terrible evils that they have to do with something particularly dark, sombre, troubling: 'It is because God *is*, that evil can assume this monstrous, unbearable and scandalous shape, as the violation of an infinite Value' (*Je est un autre*, Sillery, Anne Sigier, 1997, p. 40).

3 The notion of chance is used here as a philosophical alternative to the existence of a divine project and not as the denial of possible manifestations of pure chance occurring within this same divine project. A Creator-God could easily have given free rein to manifestations of pure chance, linked to the complexity of possible intertwinings between the countless elements inherent in his creation, at the same time drawing, as and when required, the greatest advantage for the accomplishment of his final plan. These manifestations of pure chance would then also be part of the dynamism linked to his continual creative activity. They would be in line with the only desire truly worthy of a God of love in this sphere: not to carry out his creative exploration without having provided in advance for a certain margin of freedom or relative autonomy for all possible and imaginable organisms, even for matter itself.

4 The Jesuit Gustave Martelet outlines this history of atoms in a work about the many links between the development of the cosmos and of life: 'According to the experts, the essential step took place during the first three minutes of the Universe. [...] It was during these three first minutes that hydrogen and helium appeared. The genesis of atoms began as of then. [...]

Given the cooling produced by the expansion [of the Universe], the temperatures sufficient for the elaboration of light atoms were no longer enough
to produce heavier ones, which according to the [Big Bang] hypothesis
"have to" appear in their turn. Even if we absolutely discount any finalism
[purpose], we have to recognise that the appearance of galaxies and stars,
during the expansion process, serves as a counterweight to the drop in
temperature, which this expansion causes by relaxation. Only the stars
can produce these phenomenal temperatures of billions of degrees, these
enormous pressures of ten million grams per square centimetre – a train
engine in a liqueur glass – necessary to the synthesis of much heavier atoms
than the first ones that came out of the Big Bang. [...] We can understand
that such precious stars can only end up being beautiful! Their mortal
explosion sowed the universe with a mass of elements, of which living things
gradually learnt to make unexpected and truly creative use. In order for this
to happen, it was necessary for the countless new riches produced by the
stars, which Reeves called "stardust" when they passed into humans, to be
collected [...] in the solar system by planet Earth' (*L'évolution et la creation*,
Paris, Cerf, 1998, pp. 40, 42–43, 45).

5 Observation of the vagaries and gropings provokes the theological reflection
not to see in this promising potential the sign of a creation whose ultimate
details was determined in advance, as by Voltaire's clockmaker God. On the
contrary, it suggests the basis of creativity judged by this Creator-God to
be the most apt to offer his creative exploration a potential for complexity
and fertility, which, despite the many imperatives inherent in the crossing
of certain essential thresholds of complexity, would give him the greatest
possible scope for achieving the creation of a being capable of one day
sharing his divine life.

6 To those who tend to be negative about human beings or creation in
general, the history of the Universe makes an impassioned appeal to put
things in perspective, in particular, to remember that human beings come
from mere stardust and marvel all the more that evolution, which started
from almost nothing, managed to get that far. This viewpoint will also
overturn the widespread idea that human beings are negligible compared
to the immensities that surround them. The astrophysicist Hubert Reeves
does not agree: 'This is a remark I often hear. I disagree violently. Firstly,
because even if the stars are very big, their degree of organisation is tiny
compared with that of the smallest wood violet. Stellar machinery is simple.
It involves enormous energies which it uses, all in all, quite brutally. With
an infinitely weaker supporting energy, which is nevertheless integrated
into a group of highly sophisticated biochemical cycles, the violet buds,
blossoms into beautiful flowers and spreads abroad seeds that will ensure
its reproduction' (*Patience dans l'azur*, Paris, Seuil, 1981, p. 159). But the
admirable sophistication of the wood violet is nothing compared to that of
the human being, as Gustave Martelet reminds us: 'Despite the dread we
sometimes feel because of our tiny place, in mass and duration, in the world
as a whole, one thing remains undeniable: first of all, the hypercomplexity of
any living being, but a fortiori that of vertebrates, primates and humans, has
a nobility in relation to the quantitive infinity of the expanse of the universe

that cannot be ignored. Just to give the figures, the sixty-six thousand billion cells that make up the adult body of average weight are not numerically insignificant. The number of neurons in the human brain is even less so. If these were spread out in space, with each cell as a star, our brain would create a formation greater than two hundred thousand light years: a truly neuronal Milky Way! Of course we should not wallow in these figures but this organic complexity can enable us to resist the vertigo we might feel at the size of the Universe in comparison with ourselves. It gives us the power and the right to hold our own against the gigantic numbers' (*L'évolution et la création*, op. cit., p. 176). When talking about these dimensions, we could also mention those proper to human being, not the least of which are our degree of consciousness, our conduct of chosen interpersonal relationships and above all our capacity to love.

7 For example, earthquakes, volcanic eruptions and tidal waves (whose origin is usually seismic or volcanic) are inextricably linked to the combination of these two factors, that is to say, very high temperatures at the Earth's centre and the rigidity of the Earth's crust. These high temperatures are caused by the radioactivity of certain atoms that make up this planet and the state of the Earth's crust has made possible the development of complex life forms. Without this diversity of atoms or this ever-increasing complexity, the human species could not have appeared. As for bacteria and viruses, the former have been involved in the actual functioning of life since its beginning and the latter contribute genetic material, which may cause problems for certain cells, but which have nevertheless been involved – also since the origins of life – in the complexification of genetic modifications linked to the diversification of species. Links that are inextricable from among many others.

8 The most dangerous phenomena for humanity could be compared to what medical instructions call 'undesirable side effects'. They could not be desired by a Creator-God who loved the human race. However, they risk occurring because of the complexity of the evolutionary intertwinings linked to the functioning of living beings and their life context.

9 Among these speculations, perhaps the most common are those that imply that such a God could have created human beings in another context, but that he deliberately chose to make them endure trials and sufferings in order to educate or test them in some way. It seems difficult to see behind this kind of speculation anything but a desperate attempt to justify the state of this world, without wanting to give up the human notion of a quasi-magical divine omnipotence. Under cover of education or apprenticeship, these speculations underestimate the horror of suffering – both that of human beings and that of a God of love. Without realising what they are doing, they turn God into a sadist and a monster. That is why they are not only intolerable but strictly incompatible with a God who is love.

10 Although these references to 'mystery' are justified here, the tendency to resort to it systematically when facing the question of evil is much less so, for three precise reasons. First, this tendency usually conceals a flight from the contradictions that characterise a faith that is still dependent on a Dictator-God or a Magician-God, derived from the unconscious projection

of the infantile desire for omnipotence. Second, this tendency sometimes conceals a double anti-intellectualism. On the one hand, there is mistrust of any intellectual development because it is regarded as a form of ideology – but does not systematic recourse to the notion of mystery itself become ideological? On the other hand, there is a modern obscurantism, which tends to run down human intelligence, on the grounds that this is paying homage to divine intelligence, without realising that only the opposite attitude would really pay homage to it. The greatness of human intelligence can only pay homage to the God who created it. Moreover, it can only rejoice the heart of a God who created it with the aim that human beings might one day know and understand him better and celebrate the grandeur of his creation with him. Third, the tendency to resort systematically to the notion of mystery is sometimes presented as a model of humility, which is far from being often the case. For what is the humblest attitude? That which consists in saying: 'If I have not understood, that is because it has to be an incomprehensible mystery'? Or that which consists in saying: 'If I have not understood, perhaps it is because I have not asked the right questions or because I have not gone deeply enough into the problem'?

11 This distinction also throws light on the role of prayer of intercession. Rather than being a magic formula, the purpose of such prayer is to associate itself with the love of a God who does not force the human heart but, instead, invites it to love. This does not modify the laws of nature by waving a magic wand but stimulates the full expression of their many virtualities. If believers are free to consider that this invitation and stimulation may make the difference at any moment, they still must not forget that the consequences of such divine activity are not measurable. The complexity of the parameters involved do not allow us to interpret appearances as a God of love not listening or refusing to answer our prayer. As the apostle John reminded us in his time, such a God could only associate a request concerning love with his own activity: 'Our fearlessness towards him consists in this, that if we ask anything in accordance with his will he hears us. And if we know that he listens to whatever we ask him we know that we already possess whatever we have asked of him' (1 Jn 5:14–15.)

12 So, now one of the apparently most revolting theological statements, that God's work is 'perfect', acquires quite a different meaning. If each stage of his creation can be described as 'perfect', that does not mean that it corresponds to an ideal state, but that it is uniquely the one that was capable of leading to other stages indispensable in the fulfilment of this divine plan and, hence, one day, to the final stage of resurrection, which is supposed to correspond to a perfect state.

13 This prodigious creative ingenuity and unfailing determination respectively illustrate the form and the content of this creative project. It illustrates the form of this creative project because that prodigious creative ingenuity embodies the dynamic aspect of continual search carried out by God, who both took care to bring together the most favourable conditions for an eminently fertile complexification and constantly respected the autonomous and equally creative participation of all the created elements, whether living or not. It illustrates the content of this creative project, because this

unfailing determination expresses a divine will that never lost sight of the ardently desired goal: to do everything to make possible the emergence of a living being with a consciousness capable of learning to love and capable one day of loving God himself.

14 Vigilance and discernment are necessary in statements about God for anyone wanting to make use of certain theological nuances and subtleties, which may appear finely balanced in their eyes, but which sometimes risk re-arousing inner processes capable of paralysing the journey of those to whom these statements are addressed. So anyone making these statement must be aware of the risks of disfiguration linked to that approach, seek to anticipate them, in order to bring in other elements capable of avoiding or limiting these risks.

15 Co-author with Melanie Klein of *L'amour et la haine*, the psychoanalyst Joan Rivière replies in these terms to those who are shocked by such findings or challenge them on the grounds that they have no memory of them: 'It is useless to say that we do not retain the memory – consciousness – of these first emotional experiences, or of the adaptations that accompany and result from them. These feelings and experiences remain in our unconscious. Only a small part of the love, fear and hatred that reign there throughout our lives will ever reach our consciousness. Most of the states I have described always remain unconscious. We could call psychoanalysis the study of the motivations for human behaviour, motivations that were previously inexplicable because they were unconscious, that is, unknown to ourselves' (op. cit., p. 25).

16 Many people – especially adolescents – come to regard themselves as real monsters, when certain inklings of these drives and unconscious desires come into their consciousness. How reassuring it would be for them to learn how normal they were and positive in the long term!

17 In these reflections on guilt, the psychiatrist Marc Oraison mentions the importance for each to become reconciled with time, with the stages inherent in the human condition: 'Isn't this where the uneasiness of guilt arises? The person who does not want to consent to his or her real condition, to "take their time" [...]? People want to go too quickly' (*La culpabilité*, Paris, Seuil, 1974, p. 58). Each of us should remember that we come, originally, from dust, that we bear in us all the struggles belonging to the history of life and must therefore consent to the fact that our apprenticeship in love will take time and will never finally be over. Carl Gustav Jung himself invites us to take into account the weight, present in each of us, of the whole of history, both the history of the evolution of life and the history of past generations, as the Jungian analyst Anthony Stevens explains: 'The repeated selection of chance mutations, through hundreds of millennia and millions of generations, ended up creating the archetypical structure of the human species, its present genotype. This reality is found in the structure of the psyche as inevitably as in the anatomy of the human body. [...] The hypothesis of the collective unconscious and its component archetypes has far-reaching consequences, because it inserts dynamic psychology into the main current of biology. It tries to establish a continuity between the human psyche and the rest of organic nature. It creates a bridge between the science of experience

and the behavioural sciences' (*Jung l'oeuvre-vie*, Paris, Éditions du Félin, 1994, pp. 43–44).

18 This quotation is all the more remarkable because, however inspired they may have been, the biblical authors were still human beings with the same inner struggles as others, subject to the same risks of unconscious projections as each of us (the trace of these can sometimes be found in certain ambivalent passages, especially those concerning the interpretation of the divine will). It is not surprising that it was a man like the apostle John who dared to express such a strong conviction. It was probably his long intimate time with Christ that enabled him to overcome the influence of unconscious projections, which might have affected a possible revelation or manifestation of God.

19 According to psychoanalysis, the more or less unconscious fear that can be aroused by the intensity of these sexual and aggressive drives, as well as the indirect links formed between them in the early stages of life, largely explain the diffuse guilt felt by a certain number of people about their own sexuality (except for those, of course, who have been victims of real traumas in this area). Therefore, this guilt does not mean that the sexual drives are evil in themselves, but rather, that the unconscious remembers in some way that their development was intermingled with that of the aggressive drives of the Oedipus complex.

20 This mysterious link between the union of eternity and human love is one of the most beautiful gifts that Christian theology can make to a couple's life, because it gives them a meaning and therefore the motivation to support the renewal of the quality of their love day by day. When they keep this ultimate meaning alive in their deepest selves and renew it day after day, they no longer regard time as a formidable eroder of their feelings for one another, but as an ally. This continual renewal of what is essential – only possible over the long term – gives their love the chance to reach its highest degree of intensity.

21 The psychotherapist Michel Dansereau notes in his reflections on Sigmund Freud's views about religion: 'The mystical current [...] intrigued Freud until the end of his life. In a letter to Romain Rolland, he envies this mysticism, which enable him to decipher the human soul more easily than a psychoanalyst. A final note from his hand dated 22 August 1938, found in his desk after his death, contains these words: 'Mysticism, the obscure self-perception of the kingdom that extends beyond the ego: the id' (*Freud et l'athéisme*, Paris, Desclée de Brouwer, 1971, pp. 122–123).

22 So many misunderstandings and disputes, particularly in a marriage or family context, could be prevented from growing worse if the protagonists were more conscious that an attitude or a wounding word from their partner comes from the subjective impression that they have not received the attention, recognition or love that they expected. Rather than being a rejection of love, this reaction is really an appeal to be loved more. When for the moment they doubt the other's love, letting their heart give way to sadness and finally hit back with a wounding word or gesture, this creates a vicious circle that cannot be broken except by getting over appearances and

gently seeking the source of the hurt that drove the other to behave in that way.

23   Another biblical idea, that of divine justice, usually confused with the idea of judgment, although it is considerably different, was also often misrepresented – probably through the influence of unconscious projections being discussed here – to the point where it was spontaneously opposed to the idea of mercy. However, the words *tsedeq* and *tsedaqah*, used in the Old Testament and usually translated as 'justice', mean that, through his faithfulness and love, God re-establishes his people in a state of salvation (see Ps 98:2–3). Throughout biblical history, God thus remains faithful to his covenant by forgiving wrongs of human beings and continuing to offer them his love, despite everything (see Neh 9:16–19). That is why his justice and his mercy are so closely linked and cannot be opposed.

24   Unfortunately, this unconscious process is easy to exploit from the outside, which explains the strong impact and resonance of certain spiritual trends that are sometimes more like a sort of manipulation of consciences than a genuine theological reflection. At all times, some people have thought they were doing right by fostering the fear of God, persuaded that proclaiming his unconditional love would merely lead their hearers to commit even more evil. Not only does this approach disfigure the reciprocal love, which, according to Christian revelation, God wants with each of us – 'in love there is no room for fear, but perfect love drives out fear' (1 Jn 4:18). Above all, it shows a profound lack of understanding of human psychology. Those who find they are sincerely and intensely loved want more than ever to make life beautiful for those around them. The idea of taking pleasure in doing more evil could only be found in those who are unable to believe they are sincerely loved and have no confidence in God's love, about which they have been told. Their lack of confidence is sometimes caused precisely by the ambiguous theological statements that, even amid generally positive language about God's love, may contain certain reservations or certain conditions. These give the unconscious processes discussed here all the encouragement they need to foster and reactivate people's difficulty in believing they are worthy of being loved. Then the proclamation of divine love loses the credibility that would have enabled it to start healing the wounds at the origin of some evil that has been committed.

25   Vigilance must be exercised here not only with regard to religious education or a possible preacher, but also with regard to the biblical writers themselves. The latter must also have had their own inner conflicts, so that their humanity must have left traces in their transcription of what they thought they had understood about a mystery that also went beyond them. 'I still have many things to say to you, but you cannot bear them now', said Christ to his disciples (Jn 16:12). Divine revelation can only be set in a human history, which has its own rhythm. In this, it is like a mother who takes time to teach her child to walk. How could a God of love who was trying to reveal his mystery to humanity not take into account the limits inherent in human pilgrimage and not accompany them at their own pace along the way, thus consenting to the inevitable provisional disfigurations of his divine love?

26 Under the influence of this same narcissistic wound, the inner struggle for genuine autonomy probably plays a considerable part in certain forms of systematic repression of the question of God, of deaf indifference or sometimes astonishingly aggressive rejection of him. It is as if behind these tendencies lay the fear of losing such dearly won autonomy from the parental bond, fear of finding oneself dependent again, not this time on one's biological origin but on the Origin par excellence. The psychologist Antoine Vergote describes this difficulty, often synonymous with spiritual paralysis: 'The emotional and relational history which is a long process of emancipation naturally does not dispose us to consent to a bond which implies a definitive dependence. Memories of infantile religiosity are linked to fear of continuing in a state of premature submission' (*Religion, foi, incroyance, étude psychologique*, op. cit., p. 222). Overcoming this state of spiritual paralysis cannot take place without the progressive discovery of a form of dependence that profoundly respects the liberty of the individual and is really fulfilling – for example, mutual support in love. Both believers and non-believers might at least consider that if there really existed a divine Source of love, it would be very improbable that it would prove to be deceptive in this area.

27 It is important not to confuse this attitude with genuinely taking into account a desire coming from God, since only the advantages these people might gain seem to matter to them.

28 Proponents of this argument should be questioned in their turn: 'Are the people who are dearest to you in life dearest to you because you think they resolve all your problems and fulfil all your demands?'

29 This new viewpoint does not rely on a Magician-God, dreamt up by illusions of omnipotence, or on a Dictator-God who behaves like a puppet master, but on a God of love in constant activity who is continually knocking at each heart's door without ever imposing himself. This is a divine activity with which the believer's prayer is associated in the same hope: *that love should conquer.*

30 Of course, a kind of condescension stripped of any scornful tendency – that for example, of a kind, fatherly superiority – could, in certain cases, claim to reflect something of the compassionate attitude of a God of love towards his creature, who is serving a continual apprenticeship in life. But its systematic application to God would permanently distort any creative project, whose aim was to produce a fully adult, conscious being, capable of one day enjoying reciprocal divine–human love.

31 In the second century AD, Plotinus was the first who dared to mention any desire in God himself. He conceived it as turned inwards, that is, as a desire to love himself and himself alone and not as a desire to love another or to be loved by anyone other than himself: 'As for [God], going into himself, he loves himself, he loves his pure clarity. It is himself whom he loves. [...] In order to prove that this inclination towards himself, which is like his action, and that this immobility in himself constitutes the being he is, it is enough to suppose the contrary. If he inclines outwards, he will lose his being. Therefore the action directed towards himself is his being. He and this action are one' (*Ennéades*, VI, chapter 8, para 16).

32 According to Antoine Vergote, the abusive use of the notion of need in current language 'covers up and conceals the phenomenon being studied', including when this is the human being's desire for God: 'Properly speaking, the term need refers to the vital need of an organism. But in the psychological behaviour of "the human organism", even elementary needs, are marked by motivations that one can no longer conceive of in terms of need. [...] Neither can one conclude that there is a natural need in God [...] from the fact that God's desire is expressed in metaphors of need. Religious desire can arise within a believing attachment, but it does not have the natural character of needs' (*Religion, foi, incroyance, étude psychologique*, op. cit., pp. 37, 39).

33 Additionally, the presence of this reciprocal desire to be loved reveals the sensitivity of the hearts involved. Then it indirectly shows their respective inner beauty, which is the foundation of the beauty of their union.

34 The most painful consequences of neglecting one's own desire to be loved can often be seen when it is a question of discernment about love. How many people imagine they could be happy if only they could simply live one day with the one they love? However, if the one they love has not chosen to be concerned about their happiness in return, they will end up suffering more and more from that lack of love. Before any decisive commitment, it is important to discern whether there exists a solid reciprocity of affection, a very concrete mutual attention to the desires and expectations of each.

35 When this divine Presence is identified, as it is by Christian faith, as the source and ultimate expression of love, it becomes the source and ultimate expression of all sensibility. In order to represent this divine sensibility without disfiguring it too greatly, each of us can resort to our own human experience in this sphere. We can reflect inwardly on what we felt in the presence of the most sensitive person we have ever met. Then we can tell ourselves that the sensibility of a God of love would be even greater.

36 This integration has considerable importance within the context of a life dedicated to God, for example, in a monastic vocation, because the reciprocal love that is meant to be its chief foundation can be experienced with God alone. The more the monk realises that this divine Presence continually at his side expects to be intensely loved, the more this will become the spring where he can quench his thirst to love God with all the fibres of his being, without repressing the loving energies dormant deep within him. At this spring, he can also quench his thirst to understand the appeal God addresses to him, inviting him to commit himself to such a radical vocation in such an exclusive relationship.

37 Following the example of projection theory, what evolution theory can challenge is the representation that so many believers and unbelievers make for themselves of the activity of a Creator-God and not of the existence of this Creator-God as such (see 'Creation in Essential Stages' in Part 1 of this book).

38 Quite often this settling of scores can take an aggressive turn. It even drove Ludwig Feuerbach to call the refusal to deny God's existence 'cowardice' after the discovery of projection theory: 'It is only the inconsistency of a cowardly heart and a feeble understanding that does not progress from this

awareness to the formal negation of predicates, then on to the denial of the being upon which they are based (*L'essence du christianisme*, op. cit., p. 135). If there is cowardice, doesn't it lie, rather, in the refusal to face the limits set by the necessary distinction between the question of the representation of God and that of God's existence? If there is cowardice, doesn't it lie, rather, in the tendency to rely on projection theory to halt one's spiritual journey, instead of continuing to advance into one's own night thanks to the precious light thrown by this psychological contribution? In his time and at the heart of his own inner struggles, Blaise Pascal saw how adhesion to a certain form of atheism might mean that remarkable progress had been made but, in his eyes, the journey needs to continue for several more stages: 'Atheism, a sign of spiritual strength, but only up to a point' (*Pensées et opuscules*, Paris, Hachette, 1904, p. 431).

39 This gap can also be seen in the representation of divine love itself. Ludwig Feuerbach saw it as the projection of the love that the believer already bears in himself: 'Whatever man's thinking, whatever his feelings, so is his God: whatever value a man has, that and no more, has his God. [...] You believe in love as in a divine quality because you yourself love' (op. cit., pp. 129, 135). However, even with an exceptional potential for love, human beings in their earthly state are still at the apprenticeship stage in love, a stage that is marked by their inner darkness, their wounds, their weaknesses and limitations. If they were content to project what they had in themselves, even what was best in themselves, this would not attain the Christian representation of God, that of a love 'without darkness' (1 Jn 1:5), 'perfect' (Mt 5:48). To attain that, they would have to follow a reasoning that took what was best in themselves and then consider that God's love is even greater. But that reasoned modification would no longer be a pure and simple projection of themselves. Indeed, human beings are far from spontaneously representing such a God, unless in one way or another, they have been in contact with a text or a word that mentions this God of love. Then that would not be self-projection either, because it would be a message received from outside themselves. And even in the latter case, a conscious journey would still be necessary to free themselves progressively from the fears, doubts and other obstacles that inevitably hang round the notion of God.

40 When we stress the constructive and enlightening contribution of projection theory within an inner quest, this is also an invitation not to be afraid of it, even to rejoice that human intelligence has been able to reach such a discovery. A God of love could also only rejoice at it, because this projection theory seems able to lead us to challenge theological representations that are most liable to disfigure the mystery of his divine love!

41 This mysterious divine–human correspondence not only justifies confidence in the human capacity to live in reciprocal love with God, but also confidence in the capacity of certain human analogies legitimately to approach the mystery of divine love.

42 The great twentieth-century philosopher Paul Ricoeur was firmly convinced: 'However deep-rooted evil may be it is not as deep as goodness. And if religions have a meaning, it is to liberate the depths of goodness in humans, seek it out where it is completely buried. [...] And I think that acclaiming

goodness is the fundamental hymn' ('Libérer le fond de bonté' in *Taizé, au vif de l'espérance*, Paris, Bayard, 2002, pp. 205, 207).

43   Having observed that the difficulty of perceiving one's own inner beauty can often turn into aggression against others and against oneself, Fyodor Dostoyevsky insisted on stressing, in a dialogue that has become famous, the importance for each of us to discover our fundamental beauty: '"They are not good", Kirilov resumed suddenly, "because they don't know they are good. [...] They must learn that they are good and then they will all immediately become good, every one of them. [...] The person who teaches that all are good will end the world." – "They crucified the one who did teach it. [...] If you learned that you believe in God, you would believe in God. But because you do not yet know that you believe in God, you do not believe in him," said Nicholas Vseolodovitch, smiling' (*Les démons*, Paris, Fernand Hazan, 1963, pp. 258–259).

44   'Shoulder my yoke and learn from me, for I am gentle and humble in heart, and you will find rest for your souls. Yes, my yoke is easy and my burden light', Christ reminds us (Mt 11:29–30), as if to forbid anyone, and especially religious authorities, to use his words to crush or frighten people. That would disfigure God's love and be a manipulation of consciences, which Christ strongly warns against: 'Woe to you, scribes and Pharisees! For you lock people out of the kingdom of heaven. For you do not go in yourselves, and when others are going in, you stop them' (Mt 23:13).

45   'I know your hardships and your poverty – though you are rich.' These are the words the book of Revelation (2:9) puts into Christ's mouth. Rich in what? First of all, rich in that unconditional divine love offered to each of us, but also rich in this image of God in ourselves, this mysterious divine–human correspondence, this potential for love that opens wide the doors of intimacy with God.

46   This tendency has made a strong enough impression for many thinkers to follow Ludwig Feuerbach on this point: 'In order to enrich God, man must impoverish himself; for God to be all, man must be nothing. [...] Moreover religion denies that good is a property of human beings. Man is evil, corrupt, incapable of good; but thereby God alone is good. [...] God is the absolutely positive, the sum of all realities, man is absolutely negative, the sum of all the nullities' (*L'essence du christianisme*, op. cit., pp. 143–145, 153).

47   This manipulation of consciences is the more unacceptable because it plays on the devastating sense of guilt that dwells in the depths of the human psyche for the reasons discussed in Part 2 of this book.

48   Whatever our convictions, it is striking to note that no humanism or philosophical or religious system gives a higher status to humanity than that of being destined to be united forever to the supreme Source of love itself. No humanism, no philosophical or religious system can confer upon each word and gesture of love, filled with tenderness, a higher status than this: that of being an admirable preparation to this divine–human union, which gives them that value and savour of eternity so often glimpsed in any authentic love. Atheist humanism cannot confer such greatness upon human love, as it is imprisoned in space–time, stamped with the death and nothingness to which it dooms everyone. This atheist humanism seems to live beyond its

means when it conceals the mystery and drama of each individual death, under cover of looking to future generations, family survival or social progress in the service of humanity. Will it also repress the consequences of its own convictions, that this death and this nothingness will also engulf all the generations to come and what they have achieved, as if they had never existed?

49 In the second century St Irenaus of Lyons was already strongly convinced: '[T]he glory of God is the living human being' [*gloria dei vivens homo*] (Against Heresies, Book IV, chapter 20, para 7, Paris, Cerf, *Sources chrétiennes*, no. 100, 1965, vol. 2, p. 649).

50 It is in the order of things that an exercised spiritual potential can sometimes glimpse realities that an unexercised potential finds it hard to perceive. However, for Christian spirituality, confidence in this divine Presence is not asked to depend upon a feeling that is constantly subject to the vagaries of human subjectivity. On the one hand, the nature of this divine Presence belongs to another dimension and therefore cannot be limited to what the human condition might perceive. On the other, confidence in this divine Presence, always offered, rests in the coherence of the project and desire of a God who is love. A God who loves each human being can only want to remain close to each of us all the time. Moreover, inner life is in the order of communion and not of communication and, therefore, carries within it a call to discover with astonishment that the apparent advantages of human communication – sight, hearing and touch, which so many believers would like have at their disposal in their relationship with God – are really far inferior to what they are already offered in communion. Communication implies a body limited by space and time, as well as natural understanding subject to many misunderstandings, whereas communion offers a reciprocal divine–human love the opportunity to benefit more fully from the capacity of this divine Presence always to stay close, to understand the depths of the human heart, to offer its divine love and welcome the love it is given and all this to a degree that human communication cannot reach.

51 This biblical theme of the human being created in the image of God, which is also present in the Muslim faith, could play a crucial part in inter-religious dialogue. That is because it is able to build a bridge between the mystical approaches of humanity's two great spiritual hemispheres, that which came out of India and that from the Semitic world. Unlike Christian, Jewish and Muslim mysticism, which rely on a personified conception of the Ultimate, the fundamental intention of the chief Hindu and Buddhist mystical currents is not to go out from oneself to unite with the Other through love – ecstasy – but to descend into the depths of one's being in order to discover that one's true identity is but one with that of the Ultimate – entasy. This difference does not necessarily justify the tendency to oppose them. The viewpoint of a loving union in which each – the Creator and the creature – is aware of remaining him or herself is not opposed to the viewpoint of an 'awakening', thanks to which the human becomes aware of the fundamental correspondence–unity of their depths with the Ultimate. Could not Christian, Jewish and Muslim mystics learn to marvel that recognition of this true identity indirectly confirms the very possibility

of a loving communion between God and humans? And could not Hindu and Buddhist mystics learn to marvel that a loving union, characterised by respected otherness, indirectly confirms their experience of entasy, because it implies a human identity that, from a certain viewpoint, is more divine than it appears?

52 These two issues illustrate the deepest reason for the famous Old Testament prohibition: 'You shall not make yourself a carved image or any likeness of anything in heaven above or on earth beneath or in the waters under the earth (Ex 20:4).

53 The theologian René Laurentin says that this comparison cannot claim to rest on the Bible, in particular because of the Wisdom writings in which the divine Wisdom appears as the very presence of God to the human race: 'The Wisdom literature constantly compares and correlates woman and Wisdom. And it projects onto God the values of initiative, intuition, presence to the cosmos, the sense of life, best exemplified by woman. This line of reflection, which prepares the theology of the Holy Spirit, introduces a very important theme, because it corrects the idea that man is superior to woman, as God is to humanity' ('Marie et l'anthropologie chrétienne de la femme' in *Nouvelle Revue Théologique*, vol. 89, 1967, pp. 510–511).

54 Representations of God largely similar to these two examples were painted at the same period, i.e. during the sixteenth century. Michelangelo painted the bearded old man on the vault of the Sistine Chapel in his fresco called creation; the smiling young woman was the work of an anonymous painter in the Church of St Jacob of Urschalling (Baveria) in the form of a fresco devoted to the Trinity in which there is a feminine representation of the Holy Spirit, rare enough to be mentioned.

55 Among the reasons for this relativisation of sexual identity, we should also mention primitive Christianity's concern to promote the notion of person, that the mystery of the person should be respected, whether feminine or masculine, and also to combat the surrounding theological justifications of the practice of sacred prostitution. The theologian Olivier Clément thinks that this stage was necessary to the spiritual history of humanity: 'It was necessary to affirm, beyond the weight of biology, the mystery of the person and particularly that of woman as personal existence and not merely reproductive' (*Corps de mort et de gloire*, Paris, Desclée de Brouwer, 1995, pp. 68–69). But in his eyes this stage ought to learn in time to reintegrate elements sometimes set aside in a too reactive way: 'Recovering the "spiritual" meaning of Eros is to recover a symbolism of the divine, and firstly, of the Spirit, who should no longer be uniquely masculine but both masculine and feminine at the same time as trans-sexual' (*Le visage intérieur*, Paris, Stock, 'Monde ouvert', 1978, p. 99).

56 This is how the Jungian analyst Anthony Stevens presents Carl Gustav Jung's thinking of this subject: 'In men, the *anima*, and its symmetrical representation the *animus* in women's unconscious, are part of the innate system that evolution has given us in order to promote and maintain the heterosexual bond [...] the *animus* and the *anima* resume the innate expectations with which each sex is endowed in the face of the other. [...] Fundamentally, therefore, the archetype of the opposite sex represents the

psychic equivalent of the physical characteristics of the other sex, which all men and women bear. [...] Rather than being simply archaic vestiges, these signs are anchored in a complex dynamic, which is determinant in the organisation of the relations between the sexes and which plays a crucial symbolic part in the psychic life of the individual' (*Jung, l'oeuvre-vie,* op. cit., 1994, pp. 51, 144–145).

57 An abundant theological literature has sometimes tried to deny the importance of sexual identity by relying on two biblical quotations: Galatians 3:27–28 and Luke 20:27–36. However, that interpretation of these passages does not stand up to rigorous analysis. Once they are set back in their context, these few lines from the epistle to the Galatians do not mean that sexual identity disappears in spiritual life, but that, in Christ, men and women are not longer opposed and cease to exercise any domination over one another; they become equal and reconciled. As for the text from Luke's Gospel, Christ is speaking about human marriage bonds, and not sexual identity as such, in order to remind us that eternal union is not with another human being but with God who will be 'all in all' (1 Cor 15:28). In general, the sometimes passionate denial of the role of sexual identity or the systematic attempt to play it down do not result from objective reflection, but are symptomatic either of personal wounds, linked to an individual or, more broadly, to difficulties met in the management of certain questions about one's own sexual identity. This causes the – understandable – repression or denial of the reality, which cannot, however, become a healthy long-term human and spiritual approach.

58 Anyone who tries to imagine those dearest to them – spouse, best friend etc. – without their masculine or feminine identity, or reversing it, will quickly realise that this is practically impossible. Sexual identity is linked so closely to the real me, the irreducible mystery of the person concerned.

59 This desire to live in intense love of God indirectly reveals another possible cause in the lack of interest shown by certain believers in the use of masculine or feminine analogies in theological reflection: the nature of the relationship they have with God. In fact, if this is a relationship where a certain intimacy with God has not yet developed, to the point where it has remained on a strictly hierarchical level, almost like slave and master ('Lord, Lord, have mercy'), then it is not surprising that the sexual identity attributed to an analogous representation of God leads to little change in how this faith is experienced. The same does not go for a relationship with God that is one of friendship, because friendship does not work in the same way, either in feelings or in general attitude when it is friendship with a man or with a woman. And when it comes to a love relationship with God, then things take yet another turn, towards that which human beings were created for and which Christ continually calls for ('You shall love the Lord your God with all your heart, with all your soul and with all your mind' (Mt 23:37). Then the integration of a human way of loving into intimacy with God finds precious support in the recognition of the close link between the ways of divine love and masculine and feminine ways of loving.

60 Spiritualities that treat their faithful as if they were asexual beings are seriously lacking, not so much for the various flights from self and the

many repressions that they risk causing or permanently maintaining or the ignorance of human psychic functioning they so often display. Most of all they fail because they do not lead an inner life towards a more complete dedication to God, towards a divine–human intimacy that involves offering one's whole way of being and loving to God, not leaving out any part of oneself.

61 This fact does not take anything away from the beauty of the feminine and mother love that many spiritualities attribute to Mary, but restores it to its rightful place, that is, as itself a magnificent reflection of divine love.

62 In their respective mystical traditions, the current great religions can find many treasures and other sources of inspiration on this subject. These may help people either to open up more to a certain perspective or to deepen that which is already represented. The author of the present book has too much respect for the mystical currents coming from Hassidism (Jewish mysticism), Sufism (Muslim mysticism), Bhaktism (Hindu mysticism) and especially Tantric Buddhist mysticism to take the liberty of addressing them himself in these pages, since they are not part of his own religious tradition. As for Hassidism and Sufism, let us hear Professor Carl-Albert Keller, who is an expert in the science of religions: 'Kabbalah exploits the fact that certain fundamental concepts of Judaism appear as feminine Greatnesses, for example the Torah and the Shekinah. [...] Thus God himself is perceived as a complete being, masculine and feminine, paternal and maternal, in constant balance within himself and also having loving feelings and community impulses in his own being. [...] In the Sufi tradition, passionate love is symbolised, above all, in the semi-historical, semi-legendary person of Qays, a poet madly in love with Layla, to the point that he is nicknamed "the Mad": Majnun. Majnun is an extremely popular character that mystics in love with God like to recall. [...] In Sufism, contemplation of the Divine appearing in the beautiful face of a loved one is also a currently admitted practice. [...] "I am Majnun for him whence Layla receives her theophany (who manifests his beauty in Layla)" [a disciple of the Sufi Ni'Matullah]' (*Approche de la mystique dans les religions occidentales et orientales*, Paris, Albin Michel, 1996, pp. 294–295, 289–291). We should also mention Hindu mysticism, which in *bhakti* ('love of God') developed by the great master Ramanuja in the eleventh century, gives an important place to Shakti, who is both cosmic energy and the feminine Presence of God. The love of Shri Ramakrishna for the goddess Kali becomes ones of the most striking illustrations of this: 'I looked at her and my brain was struck by lightning – She! [...] an ocean of ineffable joy rolled within me. And to the depths of my being I was conscious of the presence of the Divine Mother.' From then on his days and nights are spent in the continual presence of the Beloved' (Romain Rolland, *La vie de Ramakrishna*, Paris, Stock, 1929, pp. 46, 49). Neither should we forget Tantrism, whose influence on Hinduism and Buddhism can be seen in the importance given to the feminine representation of the Ultimate, from which certain particular themes of Tantric Buddhism are derived: 'Tantrism presents itself as a theology of divine omnipotence (*shakti*), venerated under the aspect of a goddess. [...] Moreover a Buddha does not become one until he has been "taken by the

hand" by divine Wisdom. [...] This is the "mystical marriage", which the disciple is called upon to enter at the end of his spiritual journey. She is what inspires the disciple, guides him and opens the way to him. And it is with her that in the end his "ego" (his *purusha*, his *atman*) will unite. Buddhists who deny the existence of the *atman* substitute the "discriminating power" (*vijnana*) which they marry to the supreme Wisdom (*Iprajna-Paramita*) in a strictly analogous way. [...] When the couple finally come together, the result is bliss, which Buddhists call *mah-sukha* (great happiness) and Hindus call *ananda* (spiritual joy). That is the whole programme of Tantrism' (Jean Varnne, *La tantrisme*, Paris, Albin Michel, 1997, pp. 37, 238–241).

63 The psychoanalyst Catherine Luquet-Parat invites us not to underestimate this submerged activity, which no one gets rid of altogether: 'Every endogenous or apparently exogenous difficulty revives the Oedipus conflict. This revival of the Oedipus conflict constitutes the first regressive step within a relatively stable situation [following the resolution of the Oedipus]. [...] Every new situation, each modification of the libidinal constellation, that is to say, any libidinal organisation round a new object, or in a new context, also reflects the Oedipus conflict. It all happens as if no restructuring could occur except through a new journey through the Oedipus conflict and with the help of this new journey' ('L'organisation oedipidienne du stade génital' in *Revue Française de Psychanalyse*, vol. XXXI, nos 5–6, 1967, pp. 790, 792).

64 The Dominican Dominique Cerbelaud goes so far as to write: '[Let us recall] firstly, a factor that is usually passed over in silence: in the Old Testament God is more often called "mother" than "father", notably because of the frequent use by the prophets of the image of the "womb"' ('Un Dieu d'eau et de vent, l'Esprit Saint dans les Odes de Salomon' in *La vie spirituelle*, no. 10, May–June 1994, p. 318). However, we should also point out that the use of the word *rahamin* can also refer to the feminine part present in every man, the motherly part present in every father. Olivier Clément alludes to it in a reflection on spiritual fatherhood: 'The great spiritual master is not at all de-sexed, as certain texts that are more Manichean than Christian, sometimes lead us to understand. On the contrary, if he is a man he fully realises his manhood, if she is a woman, her womanhood, as well as in some way integrating the sexual polarity, the *animus* and the *anima* of which Jung speaks. The spiritual father gains a motherly tenderness and the spiritual mother gains manly strength' (*Corps de mort et de gloire*, op. cit., p. 53).

65 These few lines of the prophet Nehemiah remain the most typical illustration of it: 'But our ancestors acted presumptuously and stiffened their necks and did not obey your commandments; they refused to obey, and were not mindful of the wonders that you performed among them; but they stiffened their necks and determined to return to their slavery in Egypt. But you are a God ready to forgive, gracious and merciful, slow to anger and abounding in steadfast love, and you did not forsake them, even when they cast an image of a calf for themselves and said, "This is your God who brought you up out of Egypt", and had committed great blasphemies, you in your great mercy did not forsake them in the wilderness; the pillar of cloud that led them in the way did not leave them by day, nor the pillar of

fire by night that gave them light on the way by which they should go' (Neh 9:16–19).

66 The synoptic Gospels (Matthew, Mark and Luke) make very limited use of the notion of father. John's Gospel is the only one to use it often, but Joachim Jeremias believes that its later composition should be taken into consideration: 'Mark, the tradition of the *logia* and the passages contained only in Luke are unanimous: in the Master's language they only know of a limited use of the word "Father" referring to God. With Matthew the usage increases, and in John "the Father" has become practically synonymous with "God". [...] Between the synoptics and John, the numbers show an amazing divergence that is very revealing. The absolute use of *ho pater* (the Father) to refer to God only goes back to a very late era' (*Abba, Jésus, et son Père*, op. cit., pp. 30, 37). About the synoptic Gospels, the theologian Elizabeth John adds: 'Moreover, other names in the language of Jesus reported by the Gospels, carry as great or even greater theological weight than the word "father". In a study of the synoptic Gospels, Elisabeth Schüssler Fiorenza [*En mémoire d'elle*, Paris, Cerf, 1986, pp. 183–200] shows that the expression usually used by Jesus to designate God, according to these texts, is *basileia tou theou*, which symbolises in a lively way the reign of God, the being of God himself establishing a community of shalom. In each of the parables and each of the sayings where Jesus uses this symbol, the one invoked is in fact God-Sophia, an inclusive model of compassion and caring. It is interesting to note: *basileia* is a feminine word' (*Dieu au-delà du masculin et du féminin Celui/Celle qui est*, Paris, Cerf, 1999, p. 133).

67 Exegetes often stress that the way in which Christ directly addresses God using the word 'Father' in the vocative already expresses a special closeness. This is no longer a simple collective designation of God as father of Israel, or even a simple statement of divine fatherhood, but a truly personal address. Following Joachim Jeremias, some theologians stress the exceptional degree of intimacy with God indicated by Jesus' use of the Aramaic term Abba – with a meaning close to 'Daddy'. According to Witold Marchel, this term was not used in Jewish prayer without a suffix or addition: 'We must distinguish between invocation in prayer and the simple affirmation of divine fatherhood. However unlikely it may seem, there is not a single Jewish text in which the single term "Abba", without suffix or addition, is employed as an invocation in prayer' (*Dieu Père dans le Nouveau Testament*, op. cit., p. 34). Following the exegete Marc Philonenko, others correct or complete that approach by inviting us not, therefore, to give free rein to pious speculations that might foster an infantilising spirituality. Rather, behind the use of the term Abba, we can see a resumption of the Aramaic version of Psalm 89, which is closely linked to Christ's recognition of his messianic identity (see his article 'De la "prière de Jésus" au "Notre Père"' in *Revue d'histoire et de philosophie religieuse*, April–June 1997, pp. 133–140). The interlocking of this unique intimacy with God and this awareness of his deepest identity finally culminates in this truly revealing assertion by Christ of his contribution to the mysterious divine reality hidden behind the word 'Father': 'He who has seen me has seen the Father' (Jn 14:9).

68 The strange absence of the mother in the parable of the 'Prodigal Son'

(see Lk 15:11–32) when not only the two sons but the servants are also mentioned, would lead us to suppose that in Christ's eyes the figure of the father already conjugates a divine fatherhood with a divine motherhood. In the seventeenth century the painter Rembrandt Harmenszoon van Rijn seems to have intuited this, as he painted the father in the parable with one masculine hand and one feminine hand in his *Return of the Prodigal Son.*

69 From the first public act of his ministry, that is, according to Luke's Gospel (4:16–21), his reading in the synagogue at Nazareth, Christ shows that he wants to erase the violent or vengeful features sometimes attributed to God, by stopping short in his reading of the book of Isaiah at words he clearly does not want to make his own. He reads: 'The Spirit of the Lord is upon me, because he has anointed me to bring good news to the poor. He has sent me to proclaim release to the captives and recovery of sight to the blind, and to let the oppressed go free, to proclaim the year of the Lord's favour.' In Isaiah (61:1–2) this is followed by a typically human disfiguration of divine love: 'and the day of vengeance of our God'.

70 Discernment – and this is probably true in all areas of life – does not consist in considering that such or such a reality is good or bad in itself – everything depends on the use that is made of it, the viewpoint adopted and the state of mind that accompanies it. According the words of Paul, discernment means having the courage to assess things for their advantages and disadvantages so as to be able, if need be, to make what is good be fruitful: 'Test everything: hold fast to what is good' (1 Th 5:21).

71 According to the psychoanalyst Melanie Klein, this ambivalence, characterised by a mixture of love and hate, has its origin in breastfeeding: 'The baby's first love and hate object, its mother, is both desired and hated with all the intensity and strength that are characteristic of primitive needs. At first the baby loves its mother when she satisfies its need to be fed, when she satisfies its hunger and gives it the sensual pleasure it feels when its mouth is stimulated by sucking the breast. [...] However, when the baby is hungry and its desires are not satisfied, or when it feels physical pain or anxiety, the situation changes abruptly. Hatred and aggression are aroused. The baby is then dominated by tendencies to destroy the very person who is the object of all its desires and who is linked in its mind to everything it experiences, both good and bad' (*L'amour et la haine*, op. cit., pp. 86–87).

72 Some may be shocked by that ambivalence or want to challenge it on the grounds that they do not have any memory of it. They should be reminded of the reply given by the psychoanalyst Joan Rivière (see note 15).

73 Certain psychoanalytic currents have sometimes identified mystical experience with an attempt to rediscover a fusional state similar to that of the child in its mother's womb. They do not hesitate to see this as a form of inner regression. In the case of Christian mysticism – the question is different in Buddhist mysticism – what is sought is not fusion, since union with God is presented as a communion, that is to say a union whose strength leaves nothing to be desired in comparison with fusion, but which takes place in respected otherness, without separation or confusion, where each is aware of remaining him or herself and in fact becoming more so.

Unlike the quest for total fusion, the fullness of communion sought by Christian mystics leads to them become most authentically themselves.

74 Using the risk of fusion with the mother as an argument to justify the refusal to use maternal analogies in theological language is to offer a solution as inappropriate, even aberrant, as it would be to suppress any bond between the child and its mother because of that same risk of fusion! Obviously a child's balance does not come about through the suppression of any link with its mother, but if possible, by the presence of a father who is careful to assume his responsibilities and harmoniously complete the mother's irreplaceable role. This essential complementarity and reciprocity is an invitation to theological reflection not to confine itself exclusively to father analogies.

75 No other biblical saying on this point is more poignant and suggestive than that of the prophet Isaiah: 'Can a woman forget her nursing child, or show no compassion for the child of her womb? Even if these may forget, yet I [God] will not forget you' (49:15).

76 Meeting this challenge indirectly allows for a more constructive use of father and mother analogies, since their exclusive use risks keeping some people to an infantilising father, as the theologian Elisabeth Parmentier notes: 'The father image of God carries with it the risk that a parent God may be added to it, who keeps believers in infantile faith: "We must rework the mother and father images of God, so that he finally becomes a God of adults and for adults. When I was a child I certainly needed a mother God and a father God. As an adult I need a deity that fits my state. [...] It is certainly not God's will that adults see themselves and always behave towards him like children" [Sigrid Grososmann, 'Gottesbilder' in *Feministische Theologie*, Stuttgart, Evangelish-Theologische Fakultät, 1988, p. 82]' (*Les filles produigues*, Geneva, Labor et Fides, 1998, p. 113).

77 In current language, the notion of person is often confused with that of individual. For Christian faith, person does not designate an isolated individual being, but 'a being in communion', a 'communion with'. This takes a radical turn when it refers to the very mystery of God. Fear of that confusion between notions of individual and person even drove the first Christian thinkers to use a different term in Greek. They preferred to speak of three 'hypostases' in God rather than three 'persons'. Later St Thomas Aquinas succeeded in formulating an approach to the concept of person in God which fully justifies its use. Perhaps this remains one of the most beautiful gifts he gave to the understanding of the faith. The Jesuit Bernard Sesboué presents this gift by stressing its novel and enlightening evocation of 'subsistent relationships' in God himself: 'In the notion of relationship, St Thomas brought out the absolute side; in the notion of person he brought out the relative side: [...] In God relationship is not like an accident inherent in a subject: it is the divine essence itself; therefore it is subsistent in the same way as the divine essence. [...] Hence divine person means the relationship as subsistent [...] (Summa Theologica q.29.a.1). The divine person is thus a purely relational being, as well as being a subsistent relational being. When a man is a father, we distinguish what he is in himself and what he is for his son, a father. In him, the relationship is accidental. In

God, however, this relationship is what constitutes the person as such. The relational for-another of the person is identical with what he is in-himself. What the Father is for his Son constitutes him uniquely and in himself as Father. In other words, the Father is wholly Father, he is nothing but that, he is subsistent fatherhood. And only this subsistent relationship really distinguishes him from his Son. In everything else, he is one with him. That is how we can understand that each of the subsistent relationships should add a number to the others, without adding a number to the essence and without dividing that essence. Person as subsistent relationship is thus the single notion capable of expressing both sides of the mystery of the Trinity' (*Le Dieu de Salut*, Paris, Desclée de Brouwer, 1994, pp. 314–315).

78 If it is not already habitual for humans to think of the notion of person as distinct from that of individual, it is even less so for them to conceive of a single and unique divine essence, a single, unique God when the presence of several divine Persons loving one another is mentioned. The theologian Walter Kasper tries to make this aspect as intelligible as possible by stressing the difference between the fact of having love and being love: 'The incomprehensible difference for the human mind between human love and divine love is that humans have love whereas God is love. Because humans have love and love is not their whole essence, they are linked to others in love without becoming a single essence with them. In humans, love creates a close and deep community of persons, but not an identity of essence. On the other hand, God is love and his essence is absolutely simple and unique. That is why the three persons possess a single essence. Their unity is an essential unity and not just a community of persons. This Trinity in unity of essence is the fathomless mystery of the Trinity, which we can never rationally understand, but only make partly accessible to the believing mind' (*Le Dieu des chrétiens*, Paris, Cerf, 1985, p. 432).

79 Respect for the otherness of each of the three divine Persons in their loving union shows the capacity of this Trinitarian mystery to give full weight to both aspects – union and otherness – of any love worthy of the name. The Christian East takes the otherness of the divine Persons as its point of departure and goes on to consider their unity, whereas the Christian West starts from the oneness of the divine essence before expressing the otherness of the Persons. Both approaches have their grandeur and each in its way expresses the mystery of this divine love. But as Walter Kasper notes, the Eastern idea, which lays greater emphasis on the interpersonal dimension of the Trinity, reveals its capacity to express the mystery of love particularly well: 'We must start from the Father, as principle-without-principle of a love that spreads out from himself, which sets the Son and the Spirit as free agents as well as uniting them in this single love. If we take God's sovereign unity in love as the point of departure and unity in the Trinity, we start, not as in the dominant Latin tradition from the divine essence, but from the Father, who principally possesses the divine essence constituted by love. For love cannot be thought of except as personal or interpersonal. Hence the person cannot exist except in communication of itself to others and in being recognised by other persons. That is the reason why the divine unity

and uniqueness, especially when God is conceived in advance as personal, cannot be understood as solitude' (Ibid, pp. 431–432).

80   If we meditate on the existence of a Creator-God, we must also take into consideration the period that preceded the beginnings of his creation, especially if we are thinking about the divine essence: the argument that the carrying out of this creation or the existence of a relationship between such a God and his creation can be interpreted as a sign of love is not enough fully to realise the link between the mystery of love and a divine essence pre-existing all creation.

81   Walter Kasper presents the Trinity as a 'historical self-revelation' of God, recalling that Trinitarian theology 'is founded exclusively on God's history with humans, in the historical self-revelation of the Father through Jesus Christ in the Holy Spirit' (*Le Dieu des chrétiens*, op. cit., p. 344). Bernard Sesboué reminds those who see the recognition of the divinity of the Holy Spirit, officially affirmed at the Council of Constantinople in 381, as late speculation, remote from the original faith, that, on the contrary, it was because this had always been recognised that the need had not been felt to formulate it officially from the beginning of Christianity: 'Until towards the middle of the fourth century, the question of the divinity of the Holy Spirit was not raised. God is eminently Spirit. His breath is the very breath of God's life. That breath swept over the waters at the moment of creation: it is therefore pre-existent. It was sent to the prophets well before Christ's coming. It did not become flesh. So its divine origin was not a problem. […] For all these reasons, the divinity of the Spirit remained a peaceful possession of the faith, although its personality was not very clearly brought out. But the long series of debates about the divinity of the Son profoundly transformed that ancient problem. It is remarkable that the divinity of the Spirit was questioned around 360, at the very moment when the legitimacy of the Nicene affirmation about the Son was being imposed. It was a sort of backlash. Should everything that had just been said in the Church about the divinity of the Son be applied equally to the Spirit? (*Le Dieu du Salut*, op. cit., pp. 261–262).

82   The apostle John symbolically chooses the story of the wedding at Cana to begin his Gospel. He invites us to see in it a revealing 'sign' of Christ's identity and the deep meaning of his ministry (see Jn 2:1–12). John concludes Revelation with the same theme of the mystical marriage (see Rev 21:2–4; 22: 17 and 20). As for St Paul, he is bold enough to write: 'I feel a divine jealousy for you, for I promised you in marriage to one husband, to present you as a chaste virgin to Christ' (2 Cor 11:2).

83   Victor Dillard introduces his feelings on the subject by a prayer which many Christian might echo: 'Holy Spirit! I try to grasp you, to single you out in the divine into which I plunge. But my outstretched hand receives nothing, and I insensibly sink to my knees before the Father or bend over my familiar inner Christ. […] You are too close, I cannot know you. Lord, show me your face a little, let me see. Teach me how I cannot do without you […] You are not included in the whole life by which our Christianity lives. You are a word, a title, a complicated expression. We imagine that only scholars in divinity can understand you. […] As if you were not a person. A person like us, and

like the Father, and like the Son, exactly like them, and thus an attractive person with all its mystery of an impenetrable core and dazzling shine' (*Au Dieu inconnu*, Paris, Beauchesne, 1938, pp. 5–9).

84 The theologian Serge Bulgakov invites us to distinguish the particular way of loving belonging to each divine Person: 'There is the personal love of one human being for another, in the image of the mutual love of the equi-hypostatic persons of the Holy Trinity; for the Father loves the Son and the Holy Spirit in his own way, as the Son loves the Father and the Spirit in his own way, and the Holy Spirit loves the Father and the Son in his own way (*Le Paraclet*, Paris, Aubier, 1946, p. 324).

85 Some theological currents have sometimes alluded to the femininity in this or that reaction of Christ (see Mt 23:37) or the masculinity sometimes linked with the activity of the Spirit, but that only reinforces the parallelism that other theologians, especially from the Orthodox Church, have intuited: on the one hand, a feminine part – that Carl Gustav Jung called the *anima* – in the mystery of Christ and the mystery of men; and on the other, a masculine part – that Carl Gustav Jung called the *animus* – in the mystery of the Spirit and the mystery of women. The theologian Paul Evdokimov sees this as the basis for a truly theological anthropology: 'The different kind of individual likeness to God of men and of women comes from the fact that they are different revelations of the Father, as are the Son and the Spirit. Saint Scheeben [a German Catholic theologian] establishes this distinction by saying that Adam is the likeness of the Son (*similitudo Filii*) and Eve is the likeness of the Holy Spirit (*similitudo Spiritus Sancti*)' (*Le Mariage, sacrement de l'amour*, Paris, ELF, 1947, p. 159). This theological anthropology seems very promising, as it gets over treating Christ alone as the archetype of humanity. Of course, this mystery of Christ, through his human nature, takes up and bears every human creature, whether man or woman. But this aspect of the mystery does not mean that our thinking about the theme of humanity created 'in God's image' cannot learn to include the part played by the Holy Spirit in the mystery of creation. In the second century St Irenaus of Lyons had already taken care to do so: 'With God there have always been Word and Wisdom, the Son and the Spirit. It is through them and in them that he has done everything, freely and independently, and it is them whom he addresses when he says: "Let us make humankind in our image, according to our likeness"' (*Against Heresies*, book IV, chapter 20, para 1, Paris, Cerf, *Sources chrétiennes*, no. 100, 1965, vol. 2, p. 627).

86 Olivier Clément stresses this aspect, paying homage to the theological thought of Paul Evdokimov: 'In his approach to the divine roots and human archetypes of the masculine and feminine [...] the masculine is linked with the *Logos* [Christ] and the feminine with *Pneuma* [Spirit], who both reveal the Father in a total and reciprocal gift. Women are called to inspire, console, incarnate like the Spirit' ('Paul Ekdokimov, témoin de la beauté de Dieu' in *Contacts*, op. cit., p. 76).

87 Among so-called 'feminist' theologies, some have sometimes tried to include feminine analogies in their language about the Person of Christ, because of the imbalance. They were afraid that attribution of these analogies to the Holy Spirit would preserve the inferiority of women to men. We conclude

that the promotion of a perfect equality between Christ and the Spirit would not only be more in accord with a Trinitarian faith worthy of the name, but also better fitted to maintain a balanced discernment in the search for the best possible use of masculine and feminine analogies in theological reflection.

88 Their complementarity and reciprocity are illustrated from the first verses of the Bible, in which God creates through his Word while his Spirit sweeps over the waters. They are even more in evidence with the coming of Christ and during his lifetime (see Lk 11:49; Lk 1:15b; Lk 1:35a; Lk 2:25b–26; Lk 3:22; Lk 4:1; Lk 4:14; Lk 10:21; Acts 1:2; Mt 12:28; 1 Pet 3:18b; Jn 16:12–13a). Moreover, they conclude the Bible: 'The Spirit and the Bride say "Come! [...] Amen. come, Lord Jesus!"' (Rev 22:17 and 20).

89 We also see this tendency in the doctrine of the *Filioque*, developed by the Christian West. Unlike in the Christian East, this doctrine holds that the Holy Spirit proceeds from the Father 'and the Son' and is not capable of giving the Holy Spirit its place of reciprocity and complementarity with the Son, or of making sufficiently clear the place of the Father as the single source of the Trinity.

90 Describing his journey from atheism towards Christian faith, Olivier Clément himself recognises that he was influenced by this fact in his choice of Orthodoxy: 'I had read things, consulted my Catholic and Protestant friends. I could not see the Trinity. Only a bi-unity. They were always talking about the Father and the Son, and their love. As for the Holy Spirit, it was their bond of love, their sigh of love, their common product. Oh! there was a whole doctrine of the Holy Spirit, but I did not see the point of it, or the point of him. The Father and the Son seemed to be enough in themselves' (*L'autre soleil*, Paris, Stock, 1975, p. 131). For its part, the Christian East has always taken care to express all the interpersonal relationships within the mystery of the Trinity, respecting the place of each divine Person, as is illustrated in the icon of the Trinity painted by Andrei Roublev in the fifteenth century, representing three persons of the same appearance. (This icon was inspired by the biblical account of the visit of three mysterious personages to Abraham; but here we don't have the Michelangelo's bearded old man or beings who are exclusively masculine.) Paul Evdokimov reminds us that this icon is considered by Orthodoxy to be 'the model of iconography and of all representations of the Trinity. [Andrei Roublev] recreates the very rhythm of the life of the Trinity, its diversity that is one and the movement of love that identifies the Persons without confusing them [...] One can well understand this feeling about the icon of icons of the Holy Trinity, painted in 1425 by the monk Andrei Roublov. About five hundred years later, the "Council of a Hundred Chapters" proclaimed it as a model of iconography and of all representations of the Trinity' (*L'art de l'icône, théologie de la beauté*, Paris, Desclée de Brouwer, 1972, p. 207).

91 Rather than its activity being limited to an impersonal force, the Holy Spirit is described by Christ as the activity of a person. Only a person can give life, spiritually give birth (see Jn 3:5–8), comfort, support (see Jn 14:16–17), bear witness, teach, lead to the truth (see Jn 14:26; 15:26; 16:13), inspire (see Lk 12:11–12). Clearer still is the passage where Christ presents the

Holy Spirit as 'another Paraclete', an invitation, according to the Taizé monk Pierre-Yves Émery, to address the Holy Spirit familiarly: 'I will ask the Father and he will give you another Paraclete to be with you for ever. This is the Spirit of truth' (Jn 14:16–17). "Paraclete" means someone who helps, supports defends. "Another Paraclete", or, as Jesus is saying in other words, another myself, to accomplish a similar work, another Someone. That means that like meeting Jesus, which is the work of the Holy Spirit, Jesus introduces the Spirit as a person, whom we should think about and address familiarly' (*Le Sant-Esprit, présence de communion*, Taizé, Les presses de Taizé, 1980, p. 57). There is even a biblical passage in which the Holy Spirit speaks in the first person, using an 'I' that is usually reserved to the Father or the Son: 'While they were worshipping the Lord and fasting, the Holy Spirit said, "Set apart for me Barnabas and Saul for the work to which I have called them"' (Acts 13:2).

92 On a strictly linguistic level, certain formulations – for example 'the Spirit of the risen Christ' or 'your Holy Spirit' – risk fostering an undeniable ambiguity, which may lead the Holy Spirit to be reduced simply to a universalised Christ. Although recognition of the unique bond between Christ and the Holy Spirit, as well as their common activity, make them inseparable from one another, we must also recognise their interpersonal relationship without confusion or separation. Pierre-Yves Émery invites us to meditate on their interpersonal love, linked to their mutual love for humanity: 'In this mutual self-effacement of the incarnate Word [Christ] to the Spirit, and the Spirit to the Word our brother, what we can see is a reciprocal love: the mutual love of the Son and the Spirit, which makes them appear as serving their respective missions, a love in which, through humility, they mutually value one another. And this love concerns us intensely, because it is also their common love of us and their joint humility for our salvation. [...] Indirectly and secondly, the reciprocity we have described between the Word and the Spirit leads us to confess the Spirit as a partner of Christ in an exchange of love, which can only be inter-personal' (*Le Saint-Esprit, présence de communion*, op. cit., pp. 55, 57).

93 Patristic expert Joseph Wolinski, co-author with Bernard Sesboué of *Dieu du Salut*, reminds us that modalism was deemed incompatible with the Trinitarian faith of the first centuries: 'By modalism is meant a doctrine that more or less radically eliminates number in God in the name of monotheism. That is to say it denies the existence in God of three eternally distinct persons. We may speak of Father, Son and Holy Spirit, but these are only three different modes whereby God enters into relations with the world. It is the same single God who manifests himself with different faces. In the fourth century Basil of Caesarea was still denouncing the modalist God' (op. cit., p. 179).

94 This tendency is a good illustration of the utilitarian use of religion that may be made by someone more concerned with their own salvation than with an authentic reciprocal love of God for its own sake.

95 Elisabeth Parmentier gives a guided tour of the various suggestions by women theologians known as 'feminist' in *Les filles prodigues* (Geneva,

Labor et Fides, 1988). See also the research by Elisabeth Johnson in *Dieu au-delà du masculin et féminin, Celui/Celle qui est* (Paris, Cerf, 1999).

96 This 'close relationship' needs further investigation. For the moment it is enough to note with the theologian René Laurentin that 'Often Wisdom seems to be identified with Spirit' (Wis 1:5; 7:22–24) with remarkable synonymous parallelisms: 'And who could ever have known your will, had you not given Wisdom and sent your holy Spirit from above (9:17)? They are often assimilated or interchangeable' (*L'Esprit Saint, cet inconnu*, Paris, Fayard, 1997, p. 114).

97 Rather than being reduced to the simply literary and poetic personification of a divine attribute that prevails from its first biblical appearances, the figure of Wisdom is gradually identified with the divine Presence itself: 'The essential thing is that this Wisdom is not a thing, a doctrine, a direction, a salvation but a Person, an "I" that makes an appeal. She is thus the figure through which Yahweh presents himself and through which he wants humans to seek him' (Gerhard von Rad, *Théologie de l'Ancien Testament*, Geneva, Labor et Fides, 1963, pp. 384–385).

98 There have been several hypotheses about the origin of this feminine figure and about possible interreligious influences that might have led the biblical authors to reproduce certain features belonging to Egyptian, Phoenician or Mesopotamian goddesses like Isis, Astarte or Ishtar. But true discernment here lies in identifying the deep reasons and spiritual experiences underlying this scriptural development, as the Dominican Philippe Lefebvre invites us to do: 'It is not just a literary figure introduced to illustrate what may be difficult in the quest for wisdom. Neither is it fundamentally an occult influence from foreign religions, which only the informed scholar could have decoded. Among the Egyptians or other peoples neighbouring Israel, wisdom is often the prerogative of a goddess. Dressed in Israelite robes she might finally have won the right to appear in holy Scripture. No. If Wisdom is a feminine person, that is fundamentally because the sages experienced her in this way. They, who had so often warned against idols of all kinds, were alert enough about their own practices and modes of expression. If for centuries in various biblical books they resolutely present Wisdom as a woman, this is not because they are the unconscious transmitters of ideas from neighbouring countries. It is because there is no better way for them to describe their intimacy with the wisdom that comes from God. Of course, that does not mean that they could not have drawn inspiration from models they found in their surroundings. [...] But it is true that the Bible sages constantly and precisely deepened this reality of Wisdom as a woman with which they lived. They let themselves be guided by her. The Wisdom texts of the Bible are a kind of exposition of that mystical life' ('La Sagesse: rencontre de l'homme et de la femme' in *La vie spirituelle*, no, 731, June 1999, pp. 201–202).

99 In his commentary on 'Hold her close, and she will make you great; embrace her and she will be your pride' (Prov 4:8) and 'She anticipates those who desire her by making herself known first' (Wis 6:13) the exegete Gerhard von Rad stresses that divine Wisdom is even represented as a seductress: 'The research by Böstrum was the first to show how Wisdom wants to

act personally in an individual's life and how intimately she calls. Thus it is obvious that through her invitation, Wisdom is the positive partner of Aphrodite Parakyptusa. Just as women who serve the goddess of voluptuousness publicly invite men to approach them to offer their chastity as a sacrifice, Wisdom attracts and seduces men and invites them to a meal which becomes a wedding feast' (*Théologie de l'Ancien Testament*, op. cit., p. 384).

100 Claude Larcher states: 'That is why certain Fathers of the Church saw her as a prefiguration not of the Word but of the Holy Spirit.' [Note the 'Word' means the Son, according to the expression of the apostle John: 'The Word became flesh and dwelt amongst us' [Jn 1:14]. He was picking up the Old Testament theme of God's 'Word' [from the masculine Hebrew word *dabar*], which was sometimes paralleled with the activity of 'Wisdom' [from the feminine Hebrew word *hokmah*]. From the second century on, St Theophilus of Antioch and St Irenaus of Lyons identified Wisdom with the Holy Spirit and not with the Son. But most of the Church Fathers did the opposite, which requires explanation. It turns out that the mysterious divine Wisdom was the only Old Testament figure, together with the no less mysterious 'Angel of Yahweh' to be described as being God and at the same time distinct from God. In this respect, it was a figure that Christian thought could theoretically connect as well with the Holy Spirit as with the Son. If we take into account the strict monotheism of Israel, it surely was not yet a divine hypostasis comparable to the hypostases in Christian faith or even a premonition of them. But in this Old Testament attempt to distinguish the Source in God from his divine Presence to humans, the early Christians had the only scriptural element which came close to their faith and enabled them to broach the question of Christ's true identity from Holy Scripture. There followed the quasi-systematic identification of Wisdom with the Son, to the detriment of recognition of many features that corresponded more to the Holy Spirit. That is why at the beginning of the twentieth century the theologian Serge Boulgakov suggested a rebalancing. He invited us to remember that the biblical figure of Wisdom was thought not to correspond in all respects to a single hypostasis and therefore not to choose one interpretation over and above another. Rather, we should discern the features that corresponded more with the Son and those that corresponded more with the Holy Spirit: 'There is a curious prejudice in sophiology, which is: Wisdom can only be linked to one single hypostasis, that of the Son; and by a relationship that is practically an identification. [...] If we admitted this, it would necessarily imply (as St Augustine pointed out) that the Father does not have Wisdom, and nor does the Holy Spirit, although it is the "Spirit of Wisdom". That is obviously absurd' (*La Sagesse de Dieu*, Lausamnne, L'Âge d'Homme, 1983, p. 27). And Serge Boulgakov adds: 'The divine Sophia is not the Son alone, as she is not the Spirit alone. She is the double unity of the Son and the Spirit, the unique revelation of the Father. [...] The inseparability and inconfusability of the hypostases of the dyad mean, at the same time, the fully concrete quality of their mutual relationship. [...] The hypostases are equally necessary and irreplaceable in the Father's divine self-revelation' (*Le Paracle*, op. cit., pp. 171–172). Serge Boulgakov's

invitation to exercise discernment in considering 'the distinctive attributes
of the hypostases' (Ibid, p. 172) constitutes a first stage in perceiving more
clearly the close relation that exists between Wisdom and the Holy Spirit.
There is another point – also seldom stressed – which needs mentioning on
the subject of the common activity of the Son and the Spirit. Christ's decla-
ration that 'The Spirit of the Lord is upon me' (Lk 4:1) and the evangelist's
insistence that Jesus was 'full of the Holy Spirit' (Lk 4:1) might also lead
us to interpret his words about Wisdom (see Lk 7:35 and 11:49) not as a
simplistic identification of Christ with Wisdom but rather as a more subtle
recognition of the manifestation of the Holy Spirit through Christ's ministry.

101   Elisabeth Johnson notes that the symbol of the dove was used in Greek
       mythology for the goddess of love: 'At Jesus' baptism, in Luke's account,
       the Holy Spirit descends on him in the bodily form of a dove (Lk 3:22).
       In Greek mythology, as Ann Belford Ulanov shows, the dove was the
       emblem of Aphrodite, the goddess of love. [...] Hence the dove figure in
       Christian art associates the Holy Spirit with the vast pre-Christian tradition
       expressing divine power in the feminine. "Iconography represents the dove
       as messenger of the goddess and the Holy Spirit" [Ann Belford Ulanov,
       The Feminine in Jungian Psychology and in Christian Theology, Evanston,
       Northwestern University Press, 1971, p. 325]' (*Dieu au-delà du masculin et
       du féminin, Celui/Celle qui est*, op. cit., p. 137).

102   Various currents of Marian spirituality have sometimes led a certain popular
       faith to call the Holy Spirit Mary's husband, Jesus' father, a thesis which,
       according to Mariology expert René Laurentin, is not acceptable and shows
       a misunderstanding of the link between Mary and the Spirit: 'In order to
       rule out the Holy Spirit being regarded as husband and father, Matthew [the
       evangelist] took care to refer to it as Spirit, which is feminine in Matthew's
       original language and to signify it by the same Greek preposition *ek*, which
       he uses to signify the role of women and to distinguish it all the way from
       the role of men. [...] The particle *ek* means the role of women in the four
       generations of the genealogy (Perez and Zerah BY Thamar (Mt 1:3), Boaz
       BY Rahab Obed BY Ruth (1:5), Solomon BY the wife of Uriah (1:6).' It is
       not by chance but quite deliberate, since in verse 20 the Holy Spirit's role
       is expressed using the same feminine mode with the same particle *ek*: 'the
       child conceived in her is BY the Holy Spirit' (Mt 1:20). [...] Designating
       the transcendent Principle of this birth by a feminine name, signifying its
       role using a feminine mode, Matthew clearly rules out the Holy Spirit
       being Mary's husband and Christ's father. Thus he admirably sets the Holy
       Spirit's mode of action into the context already provided by the Bible. [...]
       He raises Mary to the height of her feminine capacity as mother' (*L'Esprit
       Saint, cet inconnu*, op. cit., pp. 139, 140, 579). René Laurentin invites us to
       rediscover this unique, extremely close link between Mary and the Spirit,
       stressing the feminine dimension of the mystery of the Spirit: '[Mary] is
       the very transparency of the Holy Spirit and the perfect intermediary of
       his inspiration, favoured by the Holy Spirit's affinities with femininity. [...]
       Mary is thus the most perfect image and icon of the Holy Spirit, who is all
       love, all gift: on the human level she is all love, all gift. [...] This likeness of
       Mary to the Holy Spirit provides the key to a thorny problem. Protestants

and Orthodox Christians, and also Cardinals Congar and Suenens, as well as H. Mühlen, blamed the Marian movement, even the Church, for substituting Mary for the Holy Spirit, of honouring unilaterally in her person titles, functions and privileges that belong to the Holy Spirit. [...] There has indeed been an imbalance in the extent to which Mary was given many titles which belong first to the Holy Spirit, without mentioning the – often forgotten – source. [...] Mary can only be understood and grasped through the Holy Spirit, to whom she is completely relative. [...] This is the way the theology of the Virgin must progress' (Ibid, pp. 588, 591). Indeed, Yves Congar had already invited us to take up that challenge and support a development in thinking about the close link that unites Mary to the Holy Spirit: 'It is a very large subject. We must be aware of the criticism addressed to us, recognise its possible justice, but also realise the closeness of the link between the Virgin Mary and the Spirit, and therefore, of a certain common role within their absolute difference of conditions. This is a serious criticism. It comes mainly from Protestants and can be summed up thus: We attribute to Mary what belongs to the Holy Spirit; we may even allow her to occupy the place of the Paraclete. Indeed we attribute to her the title and role of comforter, advocate, defender of the faith before Christ, who is a fearsome judge. Her motherhood is such that, thanks to her, we are not orphans. She reveals Jesus who, in his turn, reveals the Father. She forms Jesus in us, a role attributed to the Holy Spirit. [...] Some people call her "the soul of the Church", a title which also belongs to the Spirit. Lastly, many spiritual souls speak of Mary's presence in them, say that Mary guides their lives and that they experience this as one may experience the presence and inspiration of the Spirit' (*Je crois en l'Esprit Saint*, op. cit., p. 224). The latter point raised by Yves Congar means we must also question the interpretation of certain spiritual experiences and phenomena sometimes called 'apparitions' with the greatest respect for the convictions of each, but also honestly. Where does the identification with Mary really come from in what the believers concerned usually describe as a feminine Presence shining with light? Does this systematic identification derive from the no less systematic attribution of any feminine element to Mary and her alone, within a religious education where God is predominantly seen as masculine? That identification process then raises another just as legitimate question. Admitting the authenticity of such experiences, why could they not be the divine Presence itself, the Presence of the Holy Spirit, since in the Bible it is Wisdom that is 'more beautiful than the sun, 'a reflection of the eternal light' (Wis 7:26)?

103 Certain suggestions have sometimes raised suspicion because they risked unbalancing faith in the Trinity. For example, in Syriac theological circles of the early centuries, the stress was strongly on maternal analogies to evoke the Holy Spirit, to the detriment of other feminine analogies. The official Church then distanced itself from that approach because it gave the impression that the Spirit was on the same level as the Father, as co-source of the Trinity, even as the Father's consort, with a Trinity then following the pattern of father, mother, child. This approach was difficult to accept because it neither respected the Father as the single source of the Trinity nor the reciprocity and complementarity of the Son and the Spirit. Contrariwise,

theological thinking that stressed both paternal and maternal analogies for the Father and masculine and feminine analogies for the Son and the Spirit, remained fully compatible with the Church's official dogma, as well as contributing to its balance and radiance.

104 This discernment of reflections of divine Beauty promoted by a long line of Orthodox thinkers – including Vladimir Soloviev, Serge Boulgakov, Vlaldimir Lossky, Paul Evdokimov, Olivier Clément – is in tune with the feeling many people have that, sometimes unwittingly, they have experienced the Absolute here below through one or other of these reflections. Olivier Clément sees the power to exercise this discernment as a mark of spiritual maturity, even within a monastic vocation. '[Paul Ekdokimov and I] were one day talking about a common acquaintance, a monk who was proud of his prowess in theology: "What can one expect of him", said Paul Ekdokimov, "he has neither seen the beauty of God nor the beauty of a woman!" On the other hand a "successful" monk reaches the source, the centre of all love. As St John Climacus reports, he can celebrate God's glory in the vision of a beautiful woman's body' ('Paul Ekdokimov, témoin de la beauté de Dieu' in *Contacts*, op. cit., p. 74). St John Climacus, who was the superior of the monastery of Mount Sinai in the seventh century, had understood: once a monk is living in reciprocal love with God, which has not got much to do with religious puritanism or moralism of any sort, he becomes gradually capable of discerning here below all sorts of reflections of divine Beauty, recognising them with joy as indirect revelations of the incomparable beauty of this mysterious divine Presence which accompanies them at every moment.

105 Whatever anyone's convictions about religion, it seems undeniable that the power of the mystery of the Trinity to assume these many aspects reinforces its credibility and legitimacy when it is a question of expressing ultimate truths about a God who is love.

106 It is important that any spiritual accompanist should take care not to project his own way of conducting his relationship with God onto the person confiding in him. He must remember that the God of love himself is the only true guide. His discernment about the genuineness of the inner life concerned – and the analogies that go with it – must stress the fact – positive or negative – of growth in confidence of being loved by God and in wanting to love God, in accordance with Christ's words: 'Either make the tree good, and its fruit good; or make the tree bad, and its fruit bad; for the tree is known by its fruit' (Mt 12:33). St John of the Cross particularly warns those whom he calls 'directors of souls' when a certain degree of intimacy with God has been reached by the person being directed: 'Let these directors of souls take care that the principal agent, the guide, the mover of souls in this state is not themselves but the Holy Spirit, who never ceases to take care of them. Directors are nothing but instruments' (quoted by Dom André Gozier, in *Présence dans le silence*, Paris, Desclée de Brouwer, 1976, p. 82). On the subject of the soul that has reached what he called the 'spiritual marriage', John of the Cross adds: 'When the soul has risen to this solitude above everything, nothing can help her any more to go up higher, except the Word, her bridegroom himself. [...] What is happening in the soul in

this contemplation of marriage with her Beloved is so high and delightful that the soul cannot express it and she does not even want to talk about it. She possesses him alone, understands him alone, enjoys him alone and her delight is that this should be between them both alone' (Ibid, p. 104).

107 St Irenaus stresses the names of the Son and the Spirit as 'Word' and 'Wisdom': 'As the prophet says: "By the Word of the Lord the heavens were made, and all their hosts by his Spirit [the breath of his mouth]" (Ps 33:6). Since therefore the Word establishes, that is, gives shape and existence, whereas the Spirit disposes the variety of powers, it is right that the Son should be called Word and the Spirit be called Wisdom of God' (Démonstration de la prédication apostolique [chapter 5], Paris, Cerf, *Sources chrétiennes*, no. 406, 1995, p. 91).

108 In the Jewish mystical tradition of the Kabbalah, an interpretation of the Song of Songs relating to these intra-divine movements of love was developed at the beginning of the second millennium of our era, according to Carl-Albert Keller: 'The Kabbalah thinks of God's hidden intimate life as a process of loving exchanges and communications between the various aspects of the divine person. These aspects, which are identical with the attributes of God mentioned in the Old Testament, are called *Sefirot* (there are ten of them). These *Sefirot* are animated by constant movements that drive them towards each other, the male *Sefirot* towards the female *Sefirot*, the lower *Sefirot* towards the higher *Sefirot* and vice versa. Moreover, the Kabbalah exploits the fact that certain fundamental concepts of Judaism appear as feminine greatnesses, as for example the Torah and the Shekinah. [...] Thus God is perceived as a complete being, masculine and feminine, paternal and maternal, in constant balance within himself, as well as having loving feelings and communal impulses within his own being' (*L'approche de la mystique dans les religions occidentales et orientales*, op. cit., pp. 294–295).

109 As André Chouraqui notes in the introduction to his own translation into French of the Song of Songs: 'Few books have been more read, translated and commented on. From the ninth to the sixteenth centuries, Salfeld listed 134 commentaries, nearly all Jewish. Rosenmuller counted 116 Christian commentaries of the Song of Songs between the sixteenth and the nineteenth centuries' (*Le Cantique des cantiques, suivi des Psaumes* [translated and introduced by André Chouraqui], Paris, PUF, 1970, p. 4). From the early centuries onwards, there have been innumerable Christian commentaries. There was a fresh upsurge of them in the twelfth century, particularly under the influence of Bernard of Clairvaux, before they came to a climax in the sixteenth century in the writings of John of the Cross.

110 René Laurentin stresses this typical inversion in Wisdom literature: 'What might be shocking in God being unilaterally symbolised by a masculine principle, and humanity being co-relatively considered as feminine, is compensated for in the Bible itself. [...] Here the meaning of the marriage is reversed. It is the glory of King Solomon to have married Wisdom. [...] The Wisdom literature draws a constant parallel and correlation between woman and Wisdom. And it projects onto God the values of initiative, intuition, presence to the cosmos, feeling for life that are best exemplified

by women. That line of reflection preparing the way for the theology of the Holy Spirit introduces a final very important theme, because it corrects the idea that man is superior to woman, as God is to humanity' ('Marie et l'anthropologie chrétienne de la femme' in Nouvelle Revue Théologique, op. cit., pp. 509–511).

111   The parallelisms between the woman's search in the Song of Songs and the attitude of divine Wisdom are very striking. In the Song the woman exclaims: 'I will rise now and go about the city, in the streets and in the squares; I will seek him whom my soul loves' (Song 3:2). And about Wisdom it is said: 'At the crossroads she takes her stand; beside the gates in front of the town, at the entrance of the portals she cries out: "To you, O people, I call"' (Prov 8:2–4) and: 'For she herself searches everywhere for those who are worthy of her, benevolently appearing to them on their ways' (Wis 6:16). Moreover, there are many parallelisms between the beauty of the woman in the Song of Songs and Wisdom: 'O fairest among women […] ah, you are beautiful, my love; ah, you are beautiful! […] You are altogether beautiful, my love; there is no flaw in you!' (Song 1:8; 1:15; 4:7) These declarations make us think of those of Solomon in the book of Wisdom: 'She is more beautiful than the sun […] I desired to take her for my bride, and fell in love with her beauty […] For she is a reflection of eternal light, a spotless mirror of the working of God, and an image of his goodness' (Wis 7:29; 8:2; 7:26). The verse: 'Open to me, my sister, my love, my dove, my perfect one!' (Song 5:2) repeats expressions typical of Wisdom, who is also compared to a 'sister' (Prov 7:4) or 'love' (Wis 7:23) and expressions typical of the Spirit, of whom the dove is a symbol and perfection a quality. This perfection, which is a divine quality par excellence, is only attributed to the woman in the Song of Songs and not to her beloved. So without challenging the traditional attribution of the man's role to God, which is based on very sound arguments, these parallelisms with divine Wisdom simply indicate that such an attribution is not the only possible interpretation or the only interpretation capable of contributing to the universal scope of the Song of Songs.

112   When genuine love is experienced in all its power and beauty, it becomes for many the human experience most likely to lead them to ask about the existence of an ultimate, transcendent Reality, closely related to love. If this world only came about by chance in order to revert irremediably to dust and nothingness as if it had never existed and if the story of life was reduced to the attempt by living organisms to live as long as possible by any means, even the most cruel, where would that feeling about love's greatness come from or the ardent desire to contribute to the happiness of another besides the self, to make the loved one's happiness an absolute priority? Isn't it precisely because there exists an ultimate Reality, closely linked to the mystery of love and when they come into contact with genuine love, humans perceive a beauty and a greatness, which from the materialist point of view, is as overwhelming as it is incomprehensible?

113   From this viewpoint, anyone (man or woman) who comes out wounded and desperate from a love relationship that has gone wrong badly need someone to tell them: You can still believe and hope with all your heart

in this prodigious mystery that you felt in the experience of human love. Contrary to your impression at the moment, you have not finally lost it. It cannot be reduced to the person you were with. It is much greater than the human being that let you taste it. It has its source in God himself and in God's image in each of us. That means you will be able to experience it in future through other people, and that one day God himself will offer it to you in all its fullness.

114 From the Christian viewpoint of the resurrection, all the best things we have experienced with our nearest and dearest who have already entered the life of eternity do not stop us being sad at their death – especially if that death is unexpected and brutal. It does not stop us missing them sorely. Nevertheless, this viewpoint confirms the importance of what we have shared together and overcomes the nonsense this experience would have been if nothingness had the last word. Thinking about a loved one who has died too soon, each of us can tell ourselves when a happy memory comes to mind: 'That action and that word contributed to the development of his or her confidence in being loved and power to love, the confidence and power with which they are loving God now. So indirectly they contribute to the intensity of the happiness they are feeling now in their loving union with God.'

115 Contrary to many received ideas, because Christian theology discerns in human love what can prepare us for a divine–human union, it confers a mystical dimension upon love here below, and gives it a beauty that no philosophical vision – certainly not an atheist one – can match.

116 According to the psychoanalyst Viktor Frankl, certain moments, however fleeting, of depression, vertigo, emptiness, nothingness, in which we feel we have lost touch with reality, are often linked to an absence of meaning, which becomes increasingly distressing. That lack of meaning, which has damaging consequences for all of us, is fostered by the repression of spirituality. According to Viktor Frankl, the unconscious cannot be reduced to repressed instincts: 'Whereas Freud's unconscious is monolithic, Frankl detects another dimension in it, which is just as active. Freud reduces the unconscious to sexual drives, whereas Viktor Frankl thinks that there is a "spiritual unconscious", dominated not by the pleasure principle but by the desire for meaning, This spiritual unconscious points towards God. Viktor Frankl sees that his patients are not only suffering from sexual frustrations (Freud) or inferiority complexes (Adler). More generally, he meets people facing an "existential void", which makes them feel dizzy. Above all, neurosis reveals a suffering from lack of meaning. This leads us to believe that the most fundamental human need is not sexual fulfilment or self-esteem, but fullness of meaning. Falling back on sex is often an ersatz for a lack of meaning. If humans are beings who desire, we have to add that their desire is directed fundamentally towards a quest for meaning' (extract from the preface by Marcel Neusch to Viktor Frankl's book *Le Dieu inconscient*, Paris, Centurion 1975, p. 7).

117 Being in the presence of another person, with all that person's mystery, expectations, desire to be understood and loved requires a particular investment, an inner struggle against routine and laziness. Probably a difficult moment in the day is coming home after a day's work that

may have been full of worries and various tensions. Thirty seconds will sometimes be enough to refresh the heart with the essential before opening the door, perhaps while parking, going upstairs or up in the lift etc. That refreshment, accessible to all and adapted to the rhythm of modern life, could change a whole evening's atmosphere. Realising that nothing is more important than showing your love to the person you love, contributing to the growth of his or her confidence in being loved and being able to love, can actively sustain listening, understanding and communion with what the other person has just been through and what he or she feels and expects now. That brief but intense refreshment would thus concretely share in the flowering of a common life, while limiting the risks of ruining it by disagreeable behaviour, caused by insufficiently mastered tiredness or a fit of temper that might have been avoided.

118   Without true reciprocity in this attention to meet the expectations of the loved one, the lack of love then felt by one of the partners, linked to a sense of injustice because of the one-way efforts they have made, causes suffering that may be unacknowledged but strong enough to make life together a sad one or even make a break-up likely. Perhaps we can never repeat enough how important it is before making any decision about a serious, to exercise careful discernment to ensure the tangible manifestation of a solid emotional reciprocity, a very concrete mutual concern for each other's desires and expectations.

119   This refreshment of the essential requires a very personal commitment, which cannot rely only on forms of refreshment for both. For each person, spaces for solitude – however brief – seem to be necessary in order to repeat a 'yes' in the depths of the heart to the loved one's happiness, a 'yes' that no one can utter for anyone else. However, all the riches of inspiration and creativity belonging to love are always welcome to discover concrete forms of refreshment as a couple. Care not to be overwhelmed by many outside worries, to keep intimate moments, remains primary. The same attention should be paid to regular exchanges in order to face what either of them might not have appreciated, so as to avoid repression of wounds which risk setting off real 'timebombs'. The tone to be used and the right moment must be chosen carefully, to limit the risk that this sharing time might become a settling of scores. Personal reflection and recalling out loud their true meaning could prove beneficial: the joy of learning to love oneself, to discover oneself ever more truly, to know that love will come out stronger. Such sharing could begin by mentioning the moments that were most appreciated. Learning what has rejoiced the heart of the other also constitutes a good opportunity to love to love.

120   See 'A God who Knows Each One's Wounds' in the Part 2 of this book, particularly note 22. Seeking to understand and cure the source of hurt in the other, the suffering and disappointment that may have driven him or her to react in such and such a way, is always more constructive than just establishing objectively which of the two was right or wrong. A common apprenticeship in love goes beyond this self-justification mechanism, where each gets bogged down in vain questions: 'Who was wrong?' 'Who was

right?' or 'Who started it?'. The answers would not settle the discomfort felt – rightly or wrongly – by the other.

121 Every advance towards greater love should be welcomed not as overdue, but as a real miracle by anyone who does not forget that human beings come from dust, that they are the result of an incredible history in which life arose, then consciousness, then love. Their physical and psychological makeup bears the marks of this whole history that preceded them and enabled them to exist. A change of perspective is required. What is astonishing is not the gap between the love desired and the love experienced, but that the deepest human identity – the image of God in them – still manages, bit by bit, to forge a way through – and with – this biological and psychic base, that is inevitably influenced by everything that has formed it through hundreds of millions of years. If we remember that the human body and psyche belong to this long history of life – with its struggles and its slowness – we will look more kindly and patiently upon an apprenticeship in loving, which can only be worked within this eminently complex human dough, in intimate collaboration with it and at its own rhythm.

122 Christian theology focused on the essential, that is on everything that can support and prepare a divine–human reciprocal love, is thus able to confer tremendous value, even mystical value, to body language, stressing its ability to develop confidence in being loved and the power to love with which humans live or will live in union with God. A spirituality that denigrated body language – especially the erotic – would thereby neglect the most intense means God has given a couple mutually to transmit that confidence in being loved and to develop their respective loving energies.

123 For many young people the temptation to commit suicide is sometimes caused because they feel – rightly or wrongly – that they are not loved. They have the (usually completely subjective) impression that no one will ever choose to love them. Or they feel they can never be happy. It is as if their suffering for the moment prevented them facing one of the most essential truths: no one, absolutely no one, can know in advance what the future will bring, who will cross their paths, what kind of love they will be offered. Those who discover, sometimes much later – but from one point of view it is never too late – the person with whom they can embark on a reciprocal love are the first to declare after the event that they had long ceased to believe this could happen and they are so grateful today that they had not done the irreparable deed. Indeed, no one can claim that their confidence in being loved cannot grow if they continue their time on Earth. All the more so if they are believers: they can always grow in confidence of being sincerely loved by welcoming the love that God himself keeps offering them all the time. This is even truer for the growth of their own power to love, since this growth does not depend directly on the people around them or the outside world in general. It is an inner choice linked to the use of their individual freedom, a choice which no one else can make for them. Everyone may experience signs of affection, however tiny, on any day of their lives, which help develop the loving energies asleep in them, even if these signs take very simple forms (a smile in the street or at work may seem banal but nevertheless also contributes to that growth in love). Lastly, even if it is full

of suffering, life is worth continuing because it offers the possibility to go on contributing in one way or another, even very indirectly, to that growth in our own power to love and that of people we meet. As Mother Teresa of Calcutta often liked to say: 'We feel ourselves that what we do is just a little drop in the ocean. But if that drop of water was not in the ocean it would be missing from it.'

124 Being assured that this divine Presence always at his side knows how much he loves: such is the confidence that enables the monk not to be frustrated that he cannot see or touch it. In fact in a human relationship if body language has the basic aim of demonstrating to your partner how much she is loved, reassuring her of the intensity of the love being given to her, then this admirable role of body language is not repressed but fulfilled within a divine-human reciprocal love: a divine presence that 'tests the mind and searches the heart' (Jer 17:19) can fully enjoy at any moment the intensity of love a human being has for it, to the point where the proper role of body language attains a greater degree of fulfilment than even the most refined eroticism can reach. The intensity of feelings in a loving heart goes beyond all the means of expression, however wonderful, that human beings have at their disposal here below.

125 It seems difficult to grasp this call to lead a monastic life without taking into account one of its most enlightening foundations, that is, the presence in God himself of a double desire: the desire to be intensely loved by human beings and the desire to love them intensely himself. Is it not this desire to be loved and to love that would drive such a God, exceptionally, to set some people apart to respond to a different vocation from that of marriage, a vocation in which God and his creature can experience the joy of being loved and loving in a radical form, which is neither superior nor inferior to the other but different? In the light of the link between human love and divine–human love described in this book, it seems that these two vocations – marriage and monasticism – each has its own mystical dimension, its own beauty, its own mission and its own power to rejoice the heart of such a God, particularly when they support in one way or another that continual apprenticeship in love which constitutes the ultimate meaning of life.

126 The integration of a human way of loving into reciprocal love with God and the use of erotic analogies by most mystics are sometimes interpreted as the consequence of simple frustration. That interpretation shows a lack of understanding of the true foundations underlying this integration and this language. Or perhaps it is sometimes simply a pretext used by non-believers, who refuse to face a phenomenon they find too disturbing or even believers who themselves feel frustrated in their own inner lives. As for this integration, we simply have to admit that human beings can only love with what they are and not what they are not! Consequently, their way of expecting and offering love has to be the same whether it is a relationship with a human person or a divine Person. This takes us to the true problem hidden behind reductionist interpretations of mystical experience: recognition or non-recognition of the existence of a God of love. Whatever people's convictions, it would be a proof of intellectual honesty to recognise the coherence of the witness of mystics as to whether

this God of love exists. How could such a God, as supreme Source of love, not be capable of offering a love as beautiful as that described by the mystics? How could such a God, as supreme Source of love, not be capable of offering love that aroused a passion and enthusiasm at least as great as that aroused by human love? As for the regular use in their language of analogies with erotic connotations, no one has better explained the reasons and the relevance of this language than St Gregory of Nyssa, in the fourth century in his First Homily on the Song of Songs: 'Human nature cannot express the superabundance of divine love. So it takes as a symbol for it what is most violent of the passions we undergo, I mean the passion of love, so that we may learn from this that the soul with her eyes fixed on the Beauty of the divine nature, is overwhelmed by it just as the body is by what is like it [...] so that our soul burns "erotically" in us with the single flame of the Spirit' (quoted and translated by Olivier Clément in Sources, *Les mystiques chrétiens des origines*, op. cit., p. 159). Finally, it is legitimate to asks why such an 'illusion' as radical as that denounced by some people, could in the long term produce such happiness, such joy, such peace and such fulfilment. These have been attested by so many men and women, who, while remaining clear about the beauty of human love, have responded to a monastic vocation and remained faithful to it, despite many calls from outside. For those who admit that only intensely experienced genuine love can habitually bear such fruits, the monastic life will appear as an indirect sign, not only of God's existence but also of the quality of love offered by God. Isn't that 'good news' for all? Carl Gustav Jung replies to those who call mystical experience an 'illusion': 'Religious experience is absolute. It is in the strict sense indisputable. We can only say that we have not had such an experience and our interlocutor will reply: "Sorry, but I have." And that's the end of it. It matters little what the world thinks of religious experience. One who has had it possesses the immense treasure of something that has filled him with a source of life, meaning and beauty and which has given the world and humanity a new splendour. He has faith (*pistis*) and peace. By what criterion can such a life be called illegitimate, such an experience invalid, such faith simply an illusion? For isn't there no better truth about ultimate things than the one that helps you to live?? [...] No one can know what the ultimate things are. So we must take them as we experience them, as we live them. And if an experience helps us make our lives healthier, more beautiful, more complete, more meaningful for ourselves and those whom we love, we can calmly state: It was a grace of God' (*Psychologie et religion*, Paris, Buchet-Chastel, 1958, pp. 198–199).

127 Some mystical traditions take this transfiguration of human eroticism into language addressed to God to great lengths. If in the spiritual history of humanity many mystics have often surprised or shocked people by their words and actions, that is because they are indwelt by a love for God that does not stop at appearances and goes beyond superficial judgments to blossom in inner freedom. The freedom they use in this area may at first seem disconcerting, but in fact it is moved by their intimate conviction that any actions can become a language of love offered to God. All the dimensions of their person can be devoted to this divine–human reciprocal love.

The Jewish mysticism of the Kabbalah belongs to those mystical currents that have dared to go furthest here. The expert in science of religions, Carl-Albert Keller comments thus on certain texts in this religious tradition: 'The texts we have just quoted are very instructive because they show the total character of the mystical quest even when it is concentrated on the excitement of Eros and the feeling of love. The Jew who is sincerely devoted to the quest for God and who tries to enter inwardly into the inwardness of his Creator is not only involved with his psyche and its emotions but also with his body. He makes physical movements which help him experience the emotions that will lead him to God . Moreover, his imagination is active. He imagines that the Shekinah, the divine Presence herself is with him, "against his body" and he tries to unite with her. Lastly he adds prayer, invocation with words. In short, he uses his whole self in the quest intimately to know the Ultimate, as it presented to him by his religious tradition' (*Approche de la mystique dans les religions occidentale et orientales*, op. cit., pp. 297–298).

128   In a Christian mysticism freed from certain repressions to be found in some writers (whose ideas require sound psychoanalysis rather than theological reflection), Eros is not repressed, set aside or denigrated but 'transfigured' according to Olivier Clément's expression: 'In the monk Eros is not crushed but transformed, transfigured. That is why St John Climacus was able to write: "Let physical Eros be your model in your desire for God"' (*L'Échelle sainte*, 26e degré, 34) and again: 'Happy is he whose passion for God is no less violent than a lover's for his beloved' (ibid., 30e degré, 11) (*Corps de mort et de gloire*, op. cit., p. 53).